The WEALTH ATTRACTION™ FORMULA

How To Attract Wealth & Manifest The Life Of Your Dreams

Ann Sanfelippo

NAPLES PRESS

Editor: Bryna René Haynes, TheHeartofWriting.com
Cover design: Bryna René Haynes, TheHeartofWriting.com
Interior layout and design: Bryna René Haynes, TheHeartofWriting.com

ISBN-10:0-692-92417-5

ISBN-13:978-0-692-92417-4

DISCLAIMER: This book is for informational purposes only. No information contained on this book constitutes tax, legal, insurance or investment advice. This book should not be considered a solicitation, offer or recommendation for the purchase or sale of any securities or other financial products and services discussed herein. Readers of this book will not be considered clients of Ann Sanfelippo and/or Wealth Attraction Academy, LLC just by virtue of access to this book. Information contained herein is not intended for persons in any jurisdiction where such distribution or use would be contrary to the laws or regulations of that jurisdiction. Readers should not construe any discussion or information contained herein as personalized advice from Ann Sanfelippo and/or Wealth Attraction Academy, LLC. Readers should discuss the personal applicability of the specific products, services, strategies, or issues posted herein with a professional advisor of his or her choosing. Information throughout this book, whether stock quotes, charts, articles, or any other statement or statements regarding capital markets or other financial information, is obtained from sources which we, and our suppliers, believe reliable; but we do not warrant or guarantee the timeliness or accuracy of this information. Neither our information providers nor we shall be liable for any errors or inaccuracies, regardless of cause, or the lack of timeliness of, or for any delay or interruption in, the transmission thereof to the user. With respect to information regarding financial performance, nothing in this book should be interpreted as a statement or implication that past results are an indication of future performance.

INVESTMENT DISCLOSURE: This book is provided for informational purposes only. Investing involves the risk of loss and investors should be prepared to bear potential losses. No portion of this book is to be construed as a solicitation to buy or sell a security or the provision of personalized investment, tax or legal advice. Certain information contained in this book is derived from sources that Ann Sanfelippo and/or Wealth Attraction Academy, LLC believes to be reliable; however, Ann Sanfelippo and/or Wealth Attraction Academy, LLC does not guarantee the accuracy or timeliness of such information and assumes no liability for any resulting damages. Readers should seek advice regarding the appropriateness of investing in any securities or other financial instruments referred to in this book, website or any other message received from Ann Sanfelippo and/or Wealth Attraction Academy, LLC and should understand that statements regarding future prospects of these or other financial products may not be realized.

LEGAL DISCLOSURE: You are hereby advised that Ann Sanfelippo and/or Wealth Attraction Academy, LLC is not a financial advisor and is NOT providing legal or tax advice. Nothing in this book or its attachments should be interpreted by you as legal advice. For legal advice and all legal related matters, Ann Sanfelippo and/or Wealth Attraction Academy, LLC recommends that you seek the advice of a qualified attorney licensed in your state or jurisdiction.

TRADEMARK: Wealth Attraction™ is a trademark of Wealth Attraction Academy, LLC

FREE BONUS TRAINING

Discover Your Wealth Attraction™ Factor!

bit.ly/WAFBonus

WHAT IS YOUR WEALTH ATTRACTION FACTOR?

IT'S TIME TO FIND OUT!

Within you is the key to manifest your deepest desires and the true definition of wealth—an overflow of abundance, happiness, and fulfillment!

This training is the perfect complement to the information in this book! In this Master Class, Ann will help you determine if you are living at your highest vibrational frequency for success, and show you how shifting your mindset and energy can uplevel your Wealth Attraction™ Factor and help you create the life of your dreams.

TABLE *of* CONTENTS

INTRODUCTION   1

CHAPTER ONE   5
The Wealth Attraction Mindset

CHAPTER TWO   23
The Five Keys to Accelerating Wealth

CHAPTER THREE   41
Desire & Vision

CHAPTER FOUR   57
Your Expert Status

CHAPTER FIVE   67
Action

CHAPTER SIX   79
Wealth Attraction Marketing

CHAPTER SEVEN   91
Accountability

CHAPTER EIGHT   103
Celebration: The Secret Ingredient

CONTINUE YOUR
WEALTH ATTRACTION JOURNEY   111

CONNECT WITH ANN   112

SPEAKER INFORMATION   113

ABOUT THE AUTHOR   115

The WEALTH ATTRACTION™ FORMULA

How To Attract Wealth & Manifest The Life Of Your Dreams

INTRODUCTION

"People say 'I want to be rich.' The question is,
'Are you willing to do what it takes?'"
-ROBERT KIYOSAKI

DURING MY PROFESSIONAL journey, I've created some pretty amazing successes. My real estate investment business nets me six to seven figures a year in revenue. I travel the world teaching people about how to create wealth. And, through my Wealth Attraction Academy, I help entrepreneurs just like you grow their businesses in a way that supports long-term wealth creation and mind-blowing success.

You may think that this book is about moneymaking strategies and investment techniques, but that's actually not the case. You see, what I've discovered over the course of the last decade as a teacher and Wealth Attraction coach is that information alone is *not* the key to success in business. In fact, all the information in the world won't make you successful if you don't have three key elements in play: a positive, growth-oriented mindset; a strong vision; and a solid plan of action based on that vision.

In this book, you'll discover my Wealth Attraction™ Formula for Entrepreneurs, which is rooted in mindset and energy, and which—if you follow it—will shift the way you see your life, your business, and your potential for creating wealth. You'll also learn my Five Keys for Accelerating Wealth, a unique blueprint you can follow to create success in *any* field, no matter where your business currently stands. I'll also share some potent marketing tips, discuss how to work with mentors and coaches (so you never have to go it alone), and show you how to establish and leverage your expert status to build your brand and create lasting success.

Are you ready to get started?

HOW TO USE THIS BOOK

As you read this book, the most important thing you can do is keep an open mind, and be willing to take an honest look at where you are in your life, business, and wealth creation.

Each chapter in this book contains practical, actionable information that you can put to use right now to shift your mindset, take inspired action, and start creating wealth in your business. Some of the information may be new, or even strange, to you, especially the pieces on mindset, energy, and vision. If this is the case, I encourage you to set aside your preconceptions and give this new way of working a try—especially if what you've been doing up until now hasn't been working as well as you'd hoped.

You can read the entire book at once, if that's your style. However, once you've done this, I encourage you to go back and spend as much time as necessary with each chapter to be sure you get the most out of the principles, ideas, and strategies I've shared. As you read, take notes about anything that stands out to you. Ask yourself what you need to learn in order to engage with these principles fully and completely. Where can you shift your perspective to be more expansive? What can you try that you haven't tried before?

If you engage with this book with honest curiosity and a willingness to "reprogram" any unhelpful ideas you currently carry around business, wealth creation, and how work shows up in your life, I promise you will experience some massive "a-ha!" moments.

AND FINALLY ...

Never forget why you are engaged in this work. You want to create wealth through entrepreneurship because you want an amazing life. That end result—your ultimate personal vision—will be your guiding light throughout this entire process. Keep that goal in the forefront of your mind, and you will always be headed in the right direction.

My wish for you is that this book will be your springboard to begin creating wealth, health, and happiness beyond your wildest dreams. May you always remember that success is within your grasp, as long as you are willing to dream, learn, and evolve.

Abundantly,

Ann

CHAPTER ONE

The Wealth Attraction Mindset

"The way we do anything is the way we do everything."
- MARTHA BECK

WHEN I FIRST MEET with potential clients, I'm often asked questions like, "How can I stop working such long hours in my business?" "How can I stop feeling like I'm throwing time and money away?" or, "I'm working my tail off! Why am I still not earning what I want and deserve?"

The thing is, these are "symptomatic" questions. They address what's happening, but not why it's happening. Before you and I can even begin to explore the "how" of your business and wealth, we need to talk about *mindset*.

Why mindset? Because mindset is the single most important component for success in business and life.

When it comes to creating wealth, mindset supersedes knowledge, experience, and even skill. Think about it: if all we needed to be successful was knowledge, *everyone* would be creating the life of their dreams. In our internet age, knowledge is infinitely accessible and practically limitless. If you want to learn how to do something, all you have to do is Google it; in a few moments, you'll have word-class information and instruction at your fingertips.

What sets successful people apart from others isn't their knowledge or skill set (although those things certainly help). It's their *mindset*—the way they think about themselves, their businesses, and their lives.

The way mindset works is summed up in these words, attributed to Mahatma Gandhi:

Your beliefs become your thoughts.

Your thoughts become your words.

Your words become your actions.

Your actions become your habits.

Your habits become your values.

And your values become your destiny.

Because your beliefs and thoughts are at the root of every action, habit, and value in your life, your mindset affects *everything* in your reality. A positive, empowered mindset will set you up for success more surely than any education, certification, or skill set. Conversely, a negative or limited mindset will sabotage even your most valiant efforts, and keep you stuck in struggle, lack, victimhood, and the daily grind.

I created the Wealth Attraction Formula for Entrepreneurs to assist you in developing a new mindset when it comes to wealth, because your mindset sets the stage for your success. Once your mindset has shifted, you will be able to apply the tools I share—and the tools you learn from others—in new and inspired ways that actually create the results you're looking for.

YOUR CIRCLE OF INFLUENCE

In order to identify and understand your current mindset, you need to look at your circle of influence.

As Jim Rohn, the famous motivational speaker, said, "You are the average of the five people you spend the most time with."

Your *current circle of influence* is comprised of the people with whom you surround yourself every day. They are the people you learn from, emulate, and align with—the people whose energies and attitudes influence your beliefs, thoughts, and behaviors (whether you're conscious of it or not).

Your circle of influence also includes the people you grew up with. Our brains grow fastest from birth to age seven, and it's during those years that we assimilate many of our deepest "truths" (aka, beliefs) about money, success, and the way the world works.

So, as you can see, your current and past experiences have "programmed" you to believe certain things about wealth, success, work, and life. And, since beliefs are at the root of all thoughts, actions, habits, and values, what you believe about wealth and success (and about your own ability to create these things) will determine if, and how, you create it.

You hold your belief systems to be your truths. On a daily basis, your decisions are made from these truths you hold. However, your truths might not be aligned with what you want to create in your life—and, if that's the case, you will need to open yourself to the possibility that all truths are subjective, and can therefore be changed.

I grew up in the Midwest. My parents were hard workers, and wanted my brothers and me to do well for ourselves. They also held some pretty common beliefs about what "doing well" meant and what it would demand. Sayings like "You have to work hard for your money," "Money doesn't grow on trees," and "Investing is risky. It's better to have a reliable paycheck" were heard daily in our house.

It was instilled in us that we should go to school, get good grades, and get good jobs—because, in my parents' minds, a good job equaled a good life. So, I got good grades, went to college, and earned my degree. However, when I started interviewing for jobs, my prospective employers didn't want to pay me what I was told in college I could expect. Looking back, this was my first sign my belief system may have been flawed.

Just after graduation, I met my husband. He was a small business owner. We spent the next ten years together working really, *really* hard to build his business; however, it seemed we were constantly playing "catch up" from month-to-month. Some months, business would be good, and we would be happy to save some money. Then, the next month, some unexpected expense would crop up, and we would lose what we had just put into the reserves. It seemed like we were always chasing that elusive stability, living from month to month, falling deeper and deeper into debt. Our shared belief that "making money is hard work" was showing up in our reality.

Eventually, the stress over our lack of money and the poor quality of our time together led us to divorce. Suddenly, I was without a home or a job. My degree was worthless, since I hadn't done anything with it in the decade since leaving college, and I was saddled with massive debt from our shared bills. I knew a massive shift had to take place if I was going to turn this around.

In search of a new beginning, I relocated from the Midwest to Florida to stay with my parents, who had moved when I was married. Instead of searching for a nine-to-five job, I decided to focus on real estate. I already owned some properties, having taken my dad's advice to buy property right out of college. "If you're renting," he told me, "you're throwing money away."

He also suggested that I should focus on buying one or two investment properties per year. If I could put a tenant in each, let the tenant's rent pay down the mortgages, then sell the properties later for a profit, he reasoned, I would create a nice little nest egg for myself. What I found, though, was that this was a slow process with a lot of ups and downs. I had several problem tenants, and some of the properties needed major repairs, which meant that they actually *cost* money rather than made it. I knew there had to be a better way.

Frustrated, I decided to attend a few local real estate investors' meetings. I met and spoke to lots of other investors, all of whom had their own opinion of how best to play the real estate game. I left feeling even more confused. I read every book I could get my hands on, trying to piece things together on my own, to no avail.

Then, late one night, I saw an infomercial for an investment system created by a well-known real estate guru. He said I could create wealth following his simple, proven plan—and I was sold! I tried to get my friends and family to go to the training with me, but they all said, "It doesn't work. It's a scam." In the end, I went alone.

At that training, I made the decision to take a leap of faith and invest in a financial education that included a mentor. The system I bought streamlined the process of accumulating cashflowing properties and shortened the learning curve for me. Immersed in this training beside other like-minded individuals, I realized that there were different ways to think about building wealth than what I had been taught. My mentor helped me stretch my mind, and gave me a different viewpoint to consider.

People told me I'd been brainwashed. I said, "I like to think of it as being 'reprogrammed.'" I was changing my beliefs about how to make money—and that, in turn, was changing my thoughts, actions, habits, and values.

Within two years of that training, I was making a six-figure income in my real estate business. Over the next several years, my real estate profits allowed me to expand into multiple businesses and different asset classes. Now, I consistently make between six and seven figures a year from my investments.

A couple of years after my business took off, I was approached by the creators of the real estate system I used, and asked to teach about how I was able to become so successful so quickly. I've spent the last several years traveling the globe, speaking and teaching to others about how to leverage these systems and create real wealth for themselves.

Because I took a chance on an opportunity that called to me, and opened myself to a shift in my beliefs, I created my own empire—and I did it in a way that was totally aligned with who I am and what I value. More, this experience led me to my greater purpose in life, which is to inspire and motivate others to create wealth, health, and happiness while enjoying a balanced life.

Shift Your Beliefs, Shift Your Life

In order to create wealth and success, I had to look outside my current circle of influence and step into a bigger arena. Similarly, if you want to create *your* vision of wealth and success, you will need to surround yourself with people who not only support that vision, but can actually help you shift your beliefs and achieve your dreams.

The first step in developing a success-oriented mindset is to understand your current mindset and where it comes from. So, grab a piece of paper and a pen, and answer the following two questions:

1. What are my current beliefs about …
    - Money?
    - The economy?
    - What it takes to create a thriving business?
    - What it takes to create long-term, sustainable wealth?
    - What it takes to leave a legacy?

2. Where did these beliefs come from? Who gave them to me?

The response to the second question—who gave you your current belief systems—will overwhelmingly be your parents, teachers, friends, and family members. Now, be honest: were these people wealthy and successful? And, if so, were they wealthy and successful *in the same way that you want to be wealthy and successful?* If you're currently struggling to create the wealth and success you desire, the answer is probably "no."

So now, let me ask you this: is it possible that your current set of beliefs may not be the truth when it comes building wealth?

We don't let go of our truths easily. I'm not asking you to change your fundamental beliefs overnight. All I ask is that you open your mind to the possibility that there are pathways to success other than the ones you were taught. Once you do that, opportunities will start to crop up for you in all kinds of unexpected places—like that infomercial I saw on late-night TV! Be willing to flip the coin; to look at the other side of the story, and admit that you might have something to learn.

In my experience, the easiest way to become rich is to "do what the rich do." This means expanding your circle of influence to include mentors, friends, and role models who have accomplished what you want to accomplish, in the same way that you want to accomplish it. Forget those who teach from theory and logic; you need to be around people who have actually *done it*. When you're in their presence, the life and wealth you desire to create isn't just a fantasy anymore; it's attainable, and it's standing right in front of you! However, to benefit from this association, you need to set aside your ego, be willing to learn, and put aside your old "truths" and judgments to make way for new, upgraded beliefs and thoughts.

The flip side of expanding your circle of influence to include people who inspire and motivate you is that you need to let go of people who are holding you back. People who cut you down, ridicule your dreams, or simply don't believe in what you're doing are not going to help you succeed. Unless you minimize your exposure to their negativity, their attitudes will affect you and drag you down. You don't need to cut them out of your life completely (unless you want to), but move them outside of the realm of close contact.

The more time you spend around successful people, the more likely you are to take on their beliefs, and the more likely you are to be successful. This is the power of your circle of influence!

THE POWER OF YOUR "WHY"

The next step in cultivating a positive mindset is understanding your "why."

A strong "why" is your driving force. It's the reason you do what you do—the reason you want to be wealthy and successful. If you don't know your "why," it's easy to get sidetracked in life and business, or slide back into unhelpful patterns of thinking and circles of influence.

Whenever you are taken outside your comfort zone to a new thought process or a new adventure, it's going to be uncomfortable. However, if you have the anchor of your "why," you will be able to see through the confusion to the end result. A strong "why" will always be greater than your fear.

When I first left my marriage, my "why" was my desire to reinvent myself so I could feel worthy and lovable again. I was broke, deeply in debt, with no job and few prospects, living with my parents. More, I was suffering from the illusion that I needed a man to provide for me. In short, I was depressed, scared, and starting from scratch.

"I'm such a mess," I would think. "Who is ever going to love me now?"

Yes, my mindset was in the toilet. So, I had to start small. I started with the belief that, if I got out of debt, I could be successful, and therefore be lovable again. I believed that I *needed* to make money in order to get what I wanted, which was to feel valued. That was my "why"—and I committed to doing whatever it took to creating a new reality for myself.

When we simply want something, we don't often follow through. But when we *need* something, we will do whatever it takes to create it. When I shifted from *wanting* to succeed to *needing* to succeed, I started to find traction. There were no limits as to what I would try in order to create the reality I wanted—including shifting my beliefs, mindset, and circle of influence.

Of course, my "why" shifted drastically as I learned more about myself, my capabilities, and my talents. I soon learned that I didn't need to rely on a man to support me; I could be a successful, single woman and create everything I wanted on my own. Nowadays, my "why" is to be a role model for others, and to instill in them that they have the potential to be and do whatever they want. But in the beginning, I didn't have the confidence or conviction to support a "why" like that. I had to start where I was. The more I worked on my mindset, the more my "why" evolved.

There will be times when you need to shift your "why" to move forward. When I saw that late-night infomercial with my real estate mentor, part of what attracted me was the big house and shiny Ferrari in the background of the shot. I wanted those things, too! Then, my mind stepped in and said, "Why do you need a Ferrari? No one from Cudahy, Wisconsin drives a Ferrari." If I had listened, I would have talked myself out of attending that first seminar, and I would have missed out on the opportunity that catapulted me into a whole new world of success. Instead, I dug deeper, and really looked at why I needed to take this big, uncomfortable step. I *wanted* a Ferrari—but I *needed* to get out of my awful financial situation. Only then could I create the life I really wanted.

Your "why" is a vital part of your mindset because it gives you the drive you need to seek out new experiences, knowledge, and circles of influence. If you aren't 100 percent sure about your "why," it's time to do some soul searching. Only if your "why" is bigger than your fear will you get to the finish line. If it's not, you will settle for less than you really want, or sabotage yourself.

YOUR WEALTH ATTRACTION FACTOR

Darryl Anka said, "Everything is energy, and that's all there is to it. Match the frequency of the reality you want and you cannot help but get that reality. It can be no other way. This is not philosophy. This is physics."

That's not just "woo-woo" nonsense. Everything in this reality, when boiled down to its simplest form, is energy. We are created from energy.

Energy is also polarized. There's positive energy, and negative energy. We are attracted to energies that are similar to our dominant vibrations, and repel those which are in opposition.

Here's a great example: Have you ever walked into a room full of people, and immediately felt drawn to someone? Maybe that person hasn't even said a word, but somehow you know that you *need* to talk to him or her. Or, maybe you've experienced the opposite: a person could be saying all the right words, but you still get a horrible feeling inside that says, "Run away!"

Maybe it's a "gut feeling," instinct, or intuition. You might get "bad vibes" or a "good feeling" about someone. Whatever words you use, you're describing energy.

In his work, Bruce D. Schneider, PhD, identifies two kinds of energy at work in our daily lives: catabolic energy and anabolic energy. Your mindset is inextricably connected to the type of energy that you exhibit and engage with every day.

Catabolic energy is contracting and draining—the kind of energy associated with stress, and with the hormones cortisol and adrenaline. It's our instinctive "fight or flight" response— helpful when you're running away from a tiger, but not helpful for dealing with nuanced situations, or for coping with life over the long term.

Anabolic energy, on the other hand, is positive, constructive, healing, and uplifting. This is the type of energy that comes from your passion, your "why," and your inner drive to succeed. It's the energy of love, caring, and positivity, and it's associated with oxytocin (the love hormone) and endorphins.

Anabolic energy opens doors; catabolic energy closes them. Anabolic energy relies on your inner source to replenish itself; catabolic energy drains your inner reserves.

It seems obvious that a positive mindset invites anabolic energy, while a negative or struggle-oriented mindset relies on catabolic energy—and it's true. To create wealth and success, we want to elevate into anabolic energy as much as possible. However, many people don't realize how much catabolic energy is present in their daily lives. They waste energy fighting when they should be flowing.

If you feel like you're doing all the right things but still struggling for every inch of ground you gain, you may be stuck in a catabolic energy spiral.

The solution: increase your Wealth Attraction Factor!

What Is Your Wealth Attraction Factor?

Your Wealth Attraction Factor is the level of catabolic versus anabolic energy present in your daily mindset and interactions. The higher the level of anabolic energy, the higher your Wealth Attraction Factor.

Your current Wealth Attraction Factor depends on a lot of things: your attitudes about yourself and others, your automatic reactions to stress and tension, your circle of influence, and the programming you received as a child (and are still carrying). The good news is, your Wealth Attraction Factor isn't set in stone. You can strategically shift your mindset to align with where you want to be and what you want to create.[1]

In order to raise the level of anabolic energy with which you engage on a daily basis, you need to shift your thought patterns into the realm of positivity and empowerment, not just for yourself, but for everyone. When you operate from a natural state of anabolic energy, you are able to overwrite old programming and change your resonance to attract more of what you want, and less of what you don't.

[1] Learn more about your Wealth Attraction Factor and how to raise it in my free Bonus Training. Go to bit.ly/WAFBonus to listen in!

One way to do this is to pay attention to your personal development through education, meditation, and engaging with your personal spirituality in a way that makes you feel whole and connected. The more you understand the way you think, feel, and behave, the more you can change your habits, your values, and ultimately your destiny.

How Spirituality & Personal Development Influence Mindset

My personal development journey began back when I was still married. I had started a Mary Kay business to try to bring in some extra money. It was doing well, but I wasn't creating the kinds of results I really wanted. Then, the company suggested that all of its reps read *Awaken the Giant Within* by Tony Robbins.

I was floored. This was amazing stuff. I felt like a whole new world of possibility had opened up for me. When I heard that Tony was holding an "Unleash the Power Within" seminar near where I lived, I immediately registered. While there, I realized that I had been playing small in my life, and it was time to step up my game! I started listening to industry leaders like Napoleon Hill, Jim Rohn, and Zig Ziglar, among others. I couldn't get enough. I listened to their products when I was at the gym, as I was driving, and while I was working around the house. I was like a sponge, soaking up all of this new information.

As my attitude and confidence improved, my Mary Kay business soared. I became a top sales director in the company, responsible for managing and motivating my own team. This required me to step up, speak publicly, and lead meetings—something with which I had always been uncomfortable. But soon, I began to notice something: the more I worked on myself, the more I attracted people who were like me. The quality and motivation of my recruits improved, which resulted in better production for my team, which resulted in greater success for me in the business, which in turn created a whole new circle of influence. It was a total success spiral.

I also got a lot of pushback during this time. Those who weren't aligned with what I was learning and creating (including my husband) told me I was being brainwashed and coerced, and that I was out of my mind with this "woo-woo" stuff. I simply thanked them for their opinions, and stopped sharing information with them. I was on my own journey.

When my divorce happened, I experienced the polar opposite of my success spiral. I needed time to deal with my personal issues and get through the divorce, but that meant that I was less available to motivate and coach my Mary Kay team. Production went down, and my team started to unravel. The more my sales stagnated, the more my mindset shifted from empowered and positive to fearful and negative. Catabolic energy took over, and I plunged into a downward spiral that ended with my business crumbling. Years of effort, all gone in just a few months.

What I learned from this (aside from the fact that I needed to create a business that didn't rely solely on my daily efforts for its success) was that my mindset was paramount to my success. When I decided to dive into the real estate world, I drew on everything I had learned during my time with Mary Kay, especially the personal development practices I'd let slide during the stress of my divorce. Creating a success spiral was easier the second time around because I already knew the power and influence of my beliefs, thoughts, and spiritual practices on my success.

Spirituality and personal development are a huge part of cultivating a positive mindset and creating a success spiral. Why? Because this work helps you become more aware of your beliefs, actions, and motivations—and when you have an awareness of something, it's a lot easier to change it if it isn't supporting you.

Before we proceed, let me be clear: when I talk about "spirituality," I'm not necessarily talking about religion. To me, spiritual practice is about connecting with whatever forces in your life feel unconditionally loving and supportive. Those forces could be God or Goddess, but they could also be nature, your higher self or soul, the Universe, or something else altogether.

Listening to powerful speakers, spiritual leaders, and educators is just one way to jumpstart your personal development. Equally as powerful are the daily practices that connect you with yourself and where you are in this moment. If you never get quiet and still, how can you possibly hear and understand what's happening inside you?

The personal and spiritual development practices you choose to engage with will help you gain insight and knowledge about who, what, and where you are. You'll get clarity about your beliefs and your circle of influence. And you'll see where your mindset is, and isn't, supporting your growth and expansion.

My personal practice includes meditation, journaling, and quiet time. Each morning, I ask for guidance about how to live my life's purpose. I listen to guided mediations, read affirmations, and journal about how I want to apply this information to my day. This helps to keep me grounded and focused not only on what I want to accomplish, but who I want to be each day. Each evening, I journal about my day, and focus on feeling gratitude for all the positive things that have happened and the success I've created.

When we are driven to succeed, it's easy to get caught up in the "doing." There are always so many tasks to accomplish, so many things to check off our to-do lists. We are always chasing after the next big thing. However, if you're not careful, this constant striving can land you in a catabolic energy spiral that will wear you out, drag you down, and sabotage your wealth and success.

Highly successful people know that mindset influences everything, and so mindset becomes their number one priority. Daily rituals like the one I've described, tailored to your specific needs and belief system, are a great way to keep the negativity and stressors of daily life from getting you down.

Here are a few simple things you can do every day to cultivate a positive mindset and keep your beliefs, thoughts, and actions aligned with where you're going and what you want to create.

- Meditate for fifteen minutes each morning.
- Start a gratitude journal: at the end of each day, write down five things for which you're grateful.
- Read or listen to personal development books while you drive, work out, or take on other tasks.
- Listen to positive and uplifting music.

Zig Ziglar once said, "People often say that motivation doesn't last. Well, neither does bathing—that's why we recommend it daily."

A daily practice is the best way to become, and stay, at peace with yourself and the world. The trick to motivating yourself is to think about the end result every day. Imagine the best possible outcome, and then set an intention to create that.

If you've had bad or unhelpful programming running your life for twenty, thirty, or forty years, don't expect things to change in an instant. Big shifts take time and dedication. But if you continually keep working on your positive mindset, and watching the thoughts and words which create your actions and habits, you will change your destiny.

WHAT'S NEXT?

Change begins with the *energy* of choice, because energy is at the root of all things in this reality. If you want to create major, positive change in your life, you need to choose—and then act on—what you really want, instead of letting your current circumstances, your circles of influence (past or present), or your old thought patterns choose it for you. There's no magic potion here; there's no privileged, secret formula that only "lucky" people know. There's only the Universal law that says, "Like attracts like. Change your energy, and you change your entire experience."

As we've discovered, the best way to change your energy is to change your mindset. And so, mindset is the foundation of the Wealth Attraction Formula—the single most important component of your success.

In this chapter, I've given you some basic information and tools to help you understand and fine-tune your mindset. This isn't a "one-and-done" thing, though. You can't just read this chapter, decide on your "why," and move on to the next step. A mindset aligned with wealth and success requires daily maintenance and a deep commitment to yourself and your dreams.

I often say to my clients, "Life is common sense put into common practice." You can read a chapter or a passage in a book and say to yourself, "Oh, I know that." However, if you're not actually practicing it or doing it, your life will never change.

That's why the next piece of the Wealth Attraction Formula is my Five Keys to Accelerating Wealth, a system for inspired action that will take you through from inception—identifying your desire and aligning your mindset with that desire—to completion and celebration of your achievements.

Remember this key equation in the Wealth Attraction Formula:

Mindset + inspired action = major shifts in your reality!

Throughout this book, as I offer information, techniques, and strategies for building wealth and success based on my Five Keys and the Wealth Attraction Formula, you will notice that I consistently refer back to mindset. In order to manifest results with any of the information I offer, your mindset needs to be aligned with where you want to go, who you want to be, and what you want to create. So, refer back to this chapter often, check in with your "why" and your circle of influence, keep up with the daily practices that help you ... and watch your life and business start to change.

CHAPTER TWO

The Five Keys to Accelerating Wealth

*"If you do what you've always done, you'll
get what you've always gotten."*
- TONY ROBBINS

AS WE LEARNED in Chapter One, mindset is the single most important component in creating wealth. If you were to totally align your mindset with wealth, and resonate only with anabolic, positive, creative energy, you would be able to create wealth literally from nothing. You could simply attract whatever you needed by thinking about it.

However, most of us aren't quite there yet—and, as we've all discovered at one point or another in our lives, wishing and hoping (when we're not in perfect resonance) only creates frustration and disappointment—aka, unhelpful catabolic energy.

That's why, in addition to elevating your mindset, it's important to have an inspired plan of action to translate what you *want* into what you actually *create*.

Life is about choices. Changing one thing can change everything. So if you're not 100 percent over-the-moon about your work, your wealth, or the life you're creating, it's time to go a different route.

My Wealth Attraction Formula is based on the progression of thoughts and feelings into actions, habits, values, and ultimately, your destiny. Your thoughts and feelings are ultimately a product of your mindset. The Five Keys to Accelerating Wealth which you'll learn in this chapter are a system for inspired action which creates results and impacts your values. They are a way to channel your positive mindset, thoughts, and feelings into action that creates real results, in real time, in your business and life. When you implement these Five Keys fully, with an open mind and as a companion plan to your mindset work, you will notice things changing more quickly than you could have imagined. You can take what you learn in this chapter and apply it to any project you're working on, in any area of your life.

In addition, throughout this book, we will move beyond theory to apply the Five Keys to every step of my Wealth Attraction Formula. This is how I create results for my clients, and how you will learn to create more wealth, success, and fulfillment in your own life—starting right now.

DESIRE: THE FIRST KEY

Desire is the first Key to Accelerating Wealth because whenever you have a wish, dream, hope, or intention, you plant a seed from which a new reality can grow. Whether this seed will flourish or remain hidden underground depends—you guessed it—on your mindset.

From the moment we get out of bed in the morning, we are moving toward something we want, even if that something is as simple as our first sip of coffee. But our bigger desires— the desires that plant the seeds of lifelong wealth, health, and happiness—aren't always so easy to fulfill. In order for these desires to bloom into our reality, we need to make sure that our mindset and energies nourish them on both the conscious and subconscious levels.

For example, if you desire to create a seven-figure business, but your circle of influence and your programming tell you that you are not worthy of that kind of success, or that you don't have what it takes to create it, or that success as an entrepreneur only happens for twenty-somethings with trust funds, your desire will be in direct conflict with your mindset. As we know, conflict is tied to catabolic, draining energy—and this conflict between desire and belief creates a vicious cycle where your desire actually drains you and lowers your energetic resonance!

To step away from this sinkhole, you need to learn to differentiate between your true desires—those which are aligned with your soul, your heart, your Source, and your purpose in the world—and your ego's desires.

The ego is that touchy, vulnerable sense of self that prefers the safety of the status quo and programmed behaviors to the challenge of expansion and change. The ego thrives on proving itself right, and, if unchecked, can become both a raging inner critic and a fountain of negativity and fear.

Catabolic energy isn't just characterized by stress, burnout, and negativity. It's tied directly to ego. The more the ego is in play, the lower our energetic resonance. Those who live in a mostly catabolic state are deeply concerned with self-preservation, personal gain, and winning at all costs. On the other hand, those who operate in a highly-anabolic state are influenced very little by ego; instead, they have learned to listen beyond the ego's ranting to the quieter, deeper voice of the soul. This connects them directly to their internal source of anabolic energy, as well as their sense of purpose and passion.

The voice of the soul is the voice that says, "Yes, you can!" and "You are meant for this." It's the voice that speaks your deepest, truest dreams and desires—the ones that really fulfill you and move you forward.

In order to align your mindset with your desire, take the time to go within and connect with what you *really* want. (Hint: your spiritual practices will help you with this!) True, soul-based desires are often different than, or even counter to, the desires of the ego. If you're only connecting with your ego's desires— the desire to prove yourself, the desire to win at all costs, the desire to fight for survival—you may find yourself in a never-ending pursuit of "the next big thing," unable to escape the draining loop of catabolic energy and its consequences. Instead, quiet your ego, then ask your soul what your true desires are and how to manifest them.

As you do this work, don't get caught up with being "perfect." Just as your mindset won't make a 180-degree shift in a day, your true, soul-deep desires may not be clear right away, and they will certainly evolve with time. As I shared in Chapter One, when I started my wealth creation journey, my desire—my "why"—was focused around proving myself to myself and other people. I now know that this was a desire tied, at least partially, to ego and catabolic energy, but at the time it was enough to jumpstart my progress and get me moving. What kept me out of the catabolic loop was my commitment to personal growth and development. With every mindset shift, my understanding of my desires changed, and my old ways of thinking were set aside. Now, my desires are much more anabolic in nature (meaning, they are more about being than doing, and more about giving than receiving), but it took several years for that evolution to take place.

So, begin where you are. Quieting your ego takes practice and dedication. There are thousands of amazing personal development tools out there that can teach you how to engage with and move past your ego and the catabolic energy it flows, so I won't rehash them here. Just choose the tools that work best for you, use them diligently, and connect with your real desires as often and as deeply as possible.

Once you actually know what you most deeply desire at this moment, you have taken the first step toward attracting real wealth—the kind of wealth that feels fulfilling, aligned, and sustainable.

VISION: THE SECOND KEY

You are the creator of your reality, and you are 100 percent responsible for the life that you are living.

You create your reality based on your thoughts, feelings, actions, habits, and values. When those things are not guided by a positive mindset and a strong, comprehensive vision, they will create your reality based on the status quo of your baseline energy (catabolic or anabolic), your programming (aka, your conscious and subconscious beliefs), and your circle of influence.

Vision is like a target at which you can point your thoughts and mindset. It is the best possible outcome of your desires, and provides a path for your energy to follow. In other words, desire is what we want, but vision is *why* we want it.

Vision is the second Key to Accelerating Wealth because it is the foundation of all the plans you will make to consciously create success. It's more than dreaming or speculation, or even imagining. In fact, vision (at least, the kind of vision that I teach people to create) is nothing less than full alignment with the energetic vibration of your wealth, success, and fulfillment.

Chances are, you already have a vision—at least, a partial one. You have an idea in your head about what "success" will look and feel like for you, even if you don't quite know how to get there yet. But here's the thing: if you're taking action based on a partially-formed vision, you may be running yourself in circles, and inviting the catabolic energies of stress, frustration, and burnout into your reality.

The Wealth Attraction Formula is based on energy, mindset, and the Five Keys. I know that it will work for you no matter what, but if you want to create truly transformative results, you will need to take the time to identify and understand your vision before you take any further action to fulfill your desires. The more real, tangible, and clear your vision is to you, the more easily you will be able to align your mindset, energy, thoughts, feelings, and actions with it.

Get To Know Your Vision

Here are some simple questions to help you identify and shape your vision:

- If all things were possible, what would your ideal life look like? What would you be doing? Where would you be doing it?

- What are the defining qualities of your ideal life? (For example: freedom, opulence, leisure, purpose, or passion.)

- Who are you in this ideal life? What are the defining qualities of the version of you who could most fully enjoy, interact with, and accelerate this ideal life? (For example: calm, joyful, confident, or excited.)

- How would a day in your ideal life unfold?

- Who shares this ideal life with you?

Notice that these vision questions are not all about work

and business. They're about life, too, and how you want to live it! After all, what good is a thriving business if you have to sacrifice in every other area of your life to make it successful? What good is wealth if you never have time to enjoy it?

Your ideal work/life balance should be a big part of your vision. If you're not sure what this looks like, ask yourself these questions, and incorporate the answers into your vision:

- How many hours a week do you want to work?

- What does an ideal work day look like to you?

- How many vacations do you want to take each year?

- How do you want your work to flow around your family schedule?

Once you tune into the specifics of your vision, including your ideal work/life balance, put yourself directly inside it. Use all five of your senses. What does your vision look like, feel like, taste like, smell like, and sound like? Use the power of your imagination to put yourself directly in your desired reality. Do this for as long as it takes for your vision to become as real to you as where you sit right now. If it helps, write down your vision in detail, or create a vision board or other representation to capture the energy.

Allow yourself to merge with your new reality. Feel your body's vibration accelerate to match what you are creating. What you are experiencing is anabolic energy at its purest! That feeling—that vibration—is your landmark, the "X" that marks the spot where you are headed. Since you now know what it feels like to be inside your ideal life, you can more easily navigate the ground between here and there. Instead of uncharted territory, your journey into your vision will feel like going home to your favorite stomping ground.

ACTION: THE THIRD KEY

For better or worse, we are blessed with limited time on this earth—and that time tends to pass far more quickly than we'd like. How we utilize our time is one of the most important choices we make as human beings. Even when you have a deep desire and clear vision, it can be easy to slip into complacency, and put off until tomorrow what could be done today—or let a fear of failure keep you from moving forward.

Anyone can talk about setting goals and "working toward your dreams." But action steps are a means to an end. Action is your path to creating your vision, but it isn't a substitute for the vision itself, and it certainly is no replacement for a positive, growth-oriented mindset. In fact, action undertaken with an unhelpful mindset and an unclear vision will likely create more struggle and catabolic energy in your life, not less.

If you've been spinning your wheels while doing "all the right things" to create wealth, your actions are probably not aligned with your mindset, desires, and vision. Busy work and "shoulds" won't get you where you want to go. Instead, you need to look at how you can connect all of your actions to your positive mindset, your desires, and your vision for wealth.

Action, in the Wealth Attraction Formula, is not just "doing stuff." It's doing stuff that *matters*—to you, and to where you want to go.

Your actions should *always* be more than items on an endless to-do list. They should take into account your mindset, your desires, and your vision, and have a clear intended outcome. Whatever you aim to accomplish will be achieved more quickly and with a greater degree of efficiency when you act in an inspired way—meaning, your actions come from a place of soul inspiration and anabolic energy, and not your programmed thought patterns or your past circles of influence.

For example, as I shared in Chapter One, my dad suggested that I accumulate rental properties, let tenants pay the mortgages, and set aside a nest egg. It didn't work out that way for me; I was following programming that wasn't aligned with what I wanted to create. Only when I shifted my mindset, found my mentor, and took inspired action did my real estate business finally take off.

At the same time, your actions don't need to be perfect. As one of my mentors once said, "You can't perfect something if you never launch it! Something is better than nothing."

As you progress through the Wealth Attraction Formula, I will ask you to take specific actions intended to create specific results. *How* you execute these actions, though, will be up to you. It's important that each action is based in a positive mindset, and that it feels light and inspired. When your action flows from your desire and vision, it will feel easy, natural, and exciting!

Fear: The Action-Killer

Sometimes, action is scary—especially when it's attached to our deepest, most treasured vision and desires.

If you are feeling scared or unworthy, or if you're stuck in a catabolic energy spiral, you will find every excuse in the book not to take the actions that will help you create your vision. You may fall into the trap of a perfectionist mindset, tweaking every last detail but never completing anything. Or, you may keep yourself ultra-busy with uninspired actions to avoid making time for what will actually move you forward.

Some of the excuses you make for avoiding inspired action may seem perfectly rational and logical—but they are just the voice of your ego trying to override the nudges of your soul. If you listen only to your ego, you will keep yourself stuck exactly where you are.

Again, it comes back to your personal growth practices and your connection to your inner truth. Only you can know what actions are right for you, and at what time. And only you can determine whether the voice urging them is that of your ego, or your soul.

There is another way in which fear shows up in action (and in your wealth creation). This one is subtle, and hard to recognize at first. It's the *small business mindset.*

Eight out of every ten small businesses fail within the first eighteen months. That's not an encouraging success rate. Why does this happen? Well, sometimes, it's a question of poor planning and execution, but more often, it's a mindset issue.

Small business owners see themselves as specialists—the "secret sauce" to their business. They believe nobody will care more about their business than they do, and therefore, they think that they need to do it all. They devote their blood, sweat, and tears to their business, thinking that if they only work hard enough, success will come their way. They might make some money, but they almost never achieve the level of success that they desire and envision.

A small business mindset can come from early programming or someone in your circle of influence, but it is almost always based in *fear*: the fear of being unnecessary or unworthy, the fear of trusting others to support you, the fear of being wrong. This fear can undermine even the most determined actions, and will inevitably lead to a cycle of catabolic energy, burnout, and frustration. The ego gets involved, saying things like, "If I only worked harder/knew more/were more worthy, I would be successful!" or "I just can't find good help. No one can do it the way I do."

On the other hand, big business owners see themselves as visionaries. They learn the business, then do the business for just long enough to set up processes and systems so they can duplicate themselves. They know how to build a team of people who share a positive and success-aligned mindset, and operate from an anabolically-charged place of, "If I win, we all win."

This difference in mindset is crucial when it comes to identifying and executing the inspired actions you will take using the Wealth Attraction Formula. If you are working with lingering fears or a small business mentality, personal development and mindset adjustments will be even more important to you as you move forward in this work.

ACCOUNTABILITY: THE FOURTH KEY

Sometimes, as an entrepreneur, it can feel like you're creating your life in a vacuum. However, nothing could be further from the truth.

Even if you work alone in your business (right now), your circle of influence is helping to shape your mindset, thoughts, beliefs, and feelings. Remember, you are the sum of the five people with whom you spend the most time—so who are you talking to about your business? Who are you asking for advice? Who is influencing your mindset?

When you truly step back and look at the monumental role other people play in your life, it's easy to see why you need to create relationships that nurture, sustain, inspire, challenge, and improve you. The more you surround yourself with positive, uplifting, powerful people, the more likely you are to cultivate those traits within yourself.

Desire informs vision. Vision becomes reality through action. Action—particularly inspired action—moves you forward and helps you manifest your vision as a concrete reality.

But what happens when you get stuck, and don't know which

action to take? Or when you simply can't make yourself take the actions you know you should?

The fourth Key to Accelerating Wealth is *accountability*. This is the first Key that involves people beyond yourself—and, in my experience, it's one of the most powerful strategies you will ever apply to your life and business.

I have been blessed to work with many mentors and accountability partners in my life. These people are geniuses at the tops of their fields. They create leading-edge programs that challenge thousands of people to be their best, most powerful selves, and take inspired action to create their dream lives in big ways. They have become part of my circle of influence, and so they challenge me to raise my mindset, energy, and vibration to match theirs.

The biggest blessing for me about working with my mentors hasn't been the information and techniques I've learned— although those skills have empowered me to create wealth, health, and happiness beyond my wildest dreams—it's been witnessing these powerful beings in action, and discovering how they engage with their own desires and visions and take action to make their goals real in their lives.

Why We Need Accountability Partners

When I started diving into personal development and mindset work, I learned a fundamental truth about human nature: *no one* can see clearly into his or her own subconscious mind. It takes an outside perspective to trigger a deep mindset shift.

One of the hardest things in life is feeling stuck in a situation, thought pattern, or belief system that you don't like and want to change. Sometimes, your reason for being stuck is buried so deeply that you can't see it. You may have exhausted yourself trying to figure out how to make the change, and given up as stress and frustration overwhelmed you.

No matter how hard you work, or how much you learn, you will always have "blind spots" around your own deeply-rooted patterns, fears, habits, and beliefs. It takes a loving outside perspective to bring these things to your attention in a way that's both acceptable and actionable to your conscious mind.

Your mentors and accountability partners are those who aren't afraid to point out when you're sabotaging yourself and undercutting your vision for a wealthy, abundant life. They can see what you don't, simply because they're not living it like you are. They don't have years of patterning and emotions tangled up in the current situation; they aren't the "boots on the ground." And so, they can put their wisdom to work in a caring but objective way, and help you turn your vision inward to overcome your blocks and get back on track to creating your dreams.

For many of us, there is a lot of discomfort around asking for help. We dread it, put it off, and sometimes avoid it at all costs. Ironically, the help we push away is often exactly what we need in order to grow and continue manifesting our vision.

If you feel constricted around asking for help or finding a mentor, ask yourself what you're trying to prove. Are you afraid to trust someone with your vision? Is it important to you to be seen as someone who knows it all? Did you learn as a young person that asking for help makes you weak? Are you reluctant to engage with people who have created their visions more successfully than you have right now, because it stirs up feelings of jealousy or inadequacy?

If you're feeling resistance, ask yourself, "How far am I willing to go in order to create my vision for my life? Am I willing to do something that feels uncomfortable in order to get unstuck?" Chances are, if you really believe in your vision, you will do whatever it takes to get there—even if it means admitting you need help!

Nearly all of the wealthy and successful people I know work with coaches, mentors, and accountability partners. They know that there are times when it's simply impossible to figure it out on your own. Partnering with someone who knows the way to where you want to go, or is on a similar path to yours, can help you make more aligned choices, and create your dream life in the most efficient, empowered, and streamlined way possible!

Three Kinds of Partnerships

There are three kinds of partnerships you can look for when creating accountability practice: mentors, coaches, and accountability partners. Each offers different benefits. Ideally, you will have at least one of each kind of partner in your life at all times.

- *Mentors* are people who have done what you want to do, and created what you want to create. More, they have done so in a way that feels aligned with your own energy and vision. Just because someone has created great wealth doesn't mean they will be a great mentor for you. For example, if you want to create wealth through online products and passive income streams, you'll want to choose a mentor who has done precisely that, not a mentor who has built wealth through stock investments or manufacturing. Ditto when it comes to work/life balance: some people really enjoy working hard and putting in long hours, but if that's not part of your vision for creating wealth, choose a mentor who knows how to put strict boundaries around his or her time!

- *Coaches* are people who know the theory and process of creating what you want to create, but haven't necessarily done it themselves (yet). They are often two or three steps ahead of you on the road to creating wealth according to your vision, and are trained to offer valuable advice and perspectives according to established systems and processes.

- *Accountability partners* are people whose journeys are paralleling your own. They're the people in your mastermind groups, fellow business owners, and others who are at the same level of personal, spiritual, and wealth development as you are. Positive, forward-thinking accountability partners help you stick to your goals and deadlines and keep you motivated to move forward, and will allow you to do the same for them. They inspire you to show up and take inspired action even when you don't feel like it.

You will always rise to the level of those with whom you surround yourself. So, when you're looking for a mentor, coach, or accountability partner, choose people whose core traits you admire and want to cultivate within yourself. Also, be sure that your mentors and coaches are continually engaging with their own mentors and coaches! You want to work with people who are constantly learning, just as you are.

CELEBRATION: THE FIFTH KEY

If you're anything like me, you're driven. You don't stop at one mountain; you want to climb them all! One challenge is barely in your rear view mirror before you're speeding along to the next one.

When you're working hard to create wealth and success, it can be tempting to go, go, go, all the time, especially once you see your efforts starting to pay off. Since you are 100 percent responsible for creating your own reality, you might as well get to it, right?

But there's a downside to that kind of drive. When you are constantly looking to the horizon, anticipating what's next, you become blind to the good things that are already happening all around you.

Let's face it: if you're leaping hurdles and breaking the status quo to reach your goals, it would be a shame not to celebrate the milestones you've already reached!

The fifth and final Key to Accelerating Wealth is *celebration*, and it's more important to realizing your dreams than you think.

Why Celebration Rules Creation

Celebration involves presence. It involves gratitude. It involves pausing your forward push for long enough to look around and say, "Wow! Look at all these amazing things I've already created!"

Anabolic energy comes from our passion, our soul, and our Source within. It flows from within us. It's limitless. But if you don't stop to celebrate what you've created—even if your actions originated in anabolic energy and intention—you can lose track of why you are working so hard in the first place.

You can get so caught up in the work of creating your vision that the vision itself becomes secondary. If this happens, you will quickly slip into catabolic energy and become burned out and disillusioned. The success you worked so hard to manifest will start to feel like a burden instead, and your optimism will nosedive into bitterness.

On the flip side, if you take the time to enjoy the journey toward wealth and success—complete with rest stops, celebrations, and feelings of gratitude along the way—you will stay attuned to the anabolic, internally-motivated energy of your soul desires and vision.

Put another way: money, wealth, and success are worthless if you don't *enjoy* them!

Celebrating your wins doesn't have to be flamboyant or expensive—in fact, if part of your vision for success includes getting out of debt or otherwise getting a handle on your finances, costly celebrations might actually set you back and trigger a catabolic energy cycle. Celebration, in this context, simply means taking time out to acknowledge what you've accomplished as a direct result of your mindset, desire, vision, action, and accountability.

Here are a few ideas for celebrating your wins:

- Take a hot bath with candles and essential oils, or a long, hot shower. Focus on how amazing you feel about your recent accomplishments.

- Get together with friends and toast one another's accomplishments.

- Take yourself out for tea, coffee, or a meal as a treat.

- Book your dream vacation.

- Open that nice bottle of wine you've been saving for a "special occasion."

- Make a list of your successes. Post it where you can see it every day.

- Share your accomplishments with your mentor or mastermind group.

- Take a whole day off!

However you choose to acknowledge your wins, make sure you do it regularly. ("Regularly" could mean monthly, weekly, or even daily.) This will support any mindset shifts you are working on and keep you connected to your "why" for creating wealth and success.

WHAT'S NEXT?

In this chapter, you've learned the basics about the Five Keys to Accelerating Wealth. You can apply and adapt these Keys, and their corresponding actions, to anything you want to create in your life.

The Keys, being a system for action and inspiration, also underpin my entire Wealth Attraction Formula, and we will be using them throughout the rest of this book to unlock the details of the Formula and your personal wealth creation process.

In Chapter Three, we'll take a much deeper look at the first two Keys, and discover what you really want from your business—and how you can create it.

Are you ready to dive in?

CHAPTER THREE

Desire & Vision

*"Visionaries look into the future and see things
not through the lens of current reality,
but through the lens of future possibility."*
- KARA CLAYPOOL

THE FIRST TWO KEYS to Accelerating Wealth are desire and vision. But how do these factors show up in your business and life, and how do they help you attract wealth?

If your business is a ship, and you are its captain, your desire and vision are your map and compass; without them, you will have a hard time finding the most direct route to where you want to go (and, by extension, to the wealth you want to create).

WHAT DO YOU WANT FROM YOUR BUSINESS?

Desire is the first Key to Accelerating Wealth. But your desire influences more than just your personal vision, goals, and drive to succeed. It also impacts your company: your clients, your present and future employees, and every one of the decisions you make as you steer the ship of your business.

As we learned in Chapter Two, your desires—your "whys," the things that motivate you—form the foundation of your vision. They are the reasons you have chosen to do what you do; the reasons you keep doing it, day after day; and the reasons why you want to grow beyond where you are right now.

Every business owner has unique desires. Sometimes, those desires are simply to make money and create a certain lifestyle, which is where I started. Sometimes, they're more altruistic and far-reaching from the get-go. No desire is wrong, and no desire is too small. Whatever it takes to get you up and moving every day is enough to start with.

However, I will say that your desires need to evolve as you and your vision grow and develop, and as you move away from the pull of your ego and get more connected to your soul's truth. When you shift from catabolic into anabolic energy, you will begin to notice that your purpose is greater than just making money. Your desires will shift to accommodate this greater purpose, and your vision will expand accordingly.

When you are in touch with your true desires and vision, and those desires and vision are in alignment with your soul truth and supported by a positive, forward-looking mindset, success is inevitable.

On the other hand, if you lose touch with your desires, or if your desires don't grow in tandem with your personal development and mindset, you will lose touch with your passion and drive—and if you lose touch with your drive, your business (and by extension, your wealth attraction) will suffer the consequences.

That's why it's important to look closely at your two levels of vision, and learn more about what you want from your business and what you want your business to do in the world.

The Two Levels of Vision

When it comes to turning your desires into goals and actions, we need to look at it on two different levels: your *personal vision* and your *company vision.*

Both of these types of vision can be tied to the same desire or set of desires; those desires will simply manifest in different ways and on different levels depending on whether you're looking at them from a personal or a company-wide perspective. However, your personal vision should always come first, both in development and in execution. After all, it's your *life* we're talking about!

PERSONAL VISION

Your personal vision provides you with direction in all areas of your life. It's the ultimate goal you're working toward, the target toward which you're pointed like an arrow. It's the life you want to create, the way you want to show up in the world, and the way you want to be remembered by others when you're no longer here on Earth.

A strong personal vision is vital to success because it keeps you operating at your highest energetic frequency, and ensures that every action you take is in full integrity and alignment with your goals, purpose, and passion. It also ensures that your personal life, health, and relationships don't fall victim to your business, and that you can maintain the balance necessary to keep operating from a place fueled by anabolic energy and positive mindset.

If you don't have a strong personal vision to follow, you won't be able to sustain the positive, forward-looking mindset and anabolic energy you need to create real wealth and success, because the things that matter to you will end up taking a backseat to your business and other people's priorities. You'll get lost in the daily grind or find yourself spinning in circles, looking for fulfillment but never quite sure how to find it. You may even attain success, only to find out that it's not the version of success that you actually wanted.

We explored your personal vision in Chapter Two with an exercise about visioning your ideal life. Now, it's time to deepen and broaden that vision, and integrate what you've discovered with your vision for your business. Where the two merge, you'll find a sweet spot for wealth attraction!

Your Personal Vision Statement

Your personal vision statement is a few powerful sentences which sum up your desires, goals, and vision for the ideal life you want to create. It's a declaration of your intentions for your life—and, as such, includes statements not only about your monetary wealth and success, but about your environment, relationships, wealth, health, happiness, time management, and anything else that came to you in your visioning practice. It's basically the Golden Rules of your life, according to you!

Writing out your personal vision is a vital part of the Wealth Attraction Formula because it establishes concrete parameters for every decision you make in your life and business. It's not enough to have this information in your head; you need to make it real in the physical world.

So, write or type your personal vision statement on a piece of paper, and post it in a place where you can see it every day. Make it beautiful, bold, and eye-catching. Make it loud enough to cut through the noise of the daily grind.

If you're a visual or tactile person, like me, you can also create a vision board for your personal vision. I love doing vision boards! When you can give your mind images to follow, your thoughts will naturally support your manifestation and achievement in those areas.

Your vision board can be made with pictures, words, or some combination of the two. You can include income goals, inspirational quotes, and even dates you've identified for your inspired actions. It's all about what speaks to you.

COMPANY VISION

Once you've gotten crystal clear on what you want from your life as a whole, you can begin to create your company vision and get clear on what you want from your business.

A strong company vision is vital to the success of any business. It articulates the company's purpose, provides inspiration and parameters for daily operations, and sets guidelines for any future decisions the company will make.

Your company vision clarifies five things:

- Why the business exists
- Who the business serves, and how
- What the business does well
- What the business hopes to achieve
- What the business is committed to

Your company vision is the destination for the journey. It defines the brand and the business, not only for you, but for your clients and your employees (current and future). This vision doesn't have to be overly complex, but it does need to be clear. Remember, you can always add to your vision as your company and its offerings grow.

When writing your company vision statement, be sure to focus on the five vital points above—especially the second one about service. This vision statement will be the barometer by which all of your products, customer interactions, and business decisions are measured. It's the "big why" for your business— the purpose for your business's existence.

A company vision goes far beyond a strategy for making money. It's a statement about the benefit you want your business to provide for humanity. Your business, like you, operates from either catabolic or anabolic energy. When you are in service to something—your customer, an ideal, a vision for a better planet—your company will naturally operate from a higher frequency, and therefore will attract clients, employees, and other businesses that are aligned with that frequency. The clearer your company vision, the easier this process of attraction will be.

As an example, here is my company vision for my Wealth Attraction Academy:

> *The Wealth Attraction Academy is committed to being a global leader in providing the most advanced and comprehensive education possible so that participating entrepreneurs can build long-term wealth in inspired and aligned ways. We excel at the development of processes, systems, and tools which accelerate entrepreneurs' successes; these tools are offered through various channels, including our education system, coaching, and mentorship programs.*

Whenever I have a question about how to integrate a new idea, product, or service, I refer back to my company vision statement. If the new idea isn't aligned with my vision, I adapt or scrap it. After all, you can't follow a path to your dream if you keep taking every detour you see!

It's a great idea to print out your company vision and post it somewhere you (and any employees) can easily see it every day. If you have associates (like virtual assistants) who work remotely, send them a copy of the vision statement they can print out and display in their own space. This way, everyone involved in the company can support the vision through daily action.

The Power of a Clear Vision

Businesses without a strong vision struggle, flounder, and eventually fail.

This isn't an abstract concept. It's absolute fact. If you, your employees, and your clients don't have a clear idea of what you stand for, what your values are, and what actions you will consistently take to support your goals, you won't achieve the same level of connection and trust throughout the complex ecosystem which is your business.

Every business exists to support itself, make a profit, and enrich its owners and employees. But the drive toward profit is not enough to fuel the kind of targeted growth and clear decision-making that characterizes successful, vision-driven business.

Case in point: Starbucks.

Now, it's practically inconceivable these days to think of Starbucks floundering. The company is ubiquitous in every major city in the world, and the name itself is synonymous with tasty, upscale coffee. But several years ago, things very nearly took a different turn for the latte giant.

Howard Schultz, the CEO who took Starbucks public, resigned his post in 2000, but came back on board in 2008 after the company's stock values plummeted by a whopping 42 percent. During his absence, Starbucks had opened nearly 10,000 new stores, but the dreaded "corporate mentality" had taken over, replacing the company culture which had once made Starbucks so attractive.

Just days after taking back his old job, Schultz decided the best way to bring the company back from the brink was to shut down every single Starbucks in the country for an hour. He wanted to retrain baristas so that customers would once again receive the level of service and quality to which they had been accustomed before expansion had diluted the company's focus and mission. It wasn't about profits; it was about delivering the perfect cup of coffee.

The company's shareholders said, "Our competitors are going to think we've lost our minds. We are going to lose millions!" They told Schultz he couldn't do it, but he did it anyway. People started talking about how Starbucks was finally on its way out, that it was dying a slow death. And yet, although that shutdown cost the company tens of millions of dollars in the short term, it was an investment in the future of the brand.

Not only did Schultz renew Starbucks' commitment to quality coffee, he refused to listen to shareholder demands to cut back on healthcare for workers. In fact, he *expanded* health care coverage to include even part-timers, and in 2014 implemented a free college tuition program for employees in partnership with Arizona State University. These programs, although costly, made Starbucks an even more attractive place to work.

Why did this strategy succeed? Because Starbucks' company vision wasn't to provide the cheapest possible coffee to the largest possible demographic, but rather to give customers an upscale experience with a personal touch. People who go to Starbucks are willing to pay $5 for a latte because of the quality of the product and experience they receive—and that means that the employees need to be happy, fulfilled, and excited enough about their jobs to provide that level of service. Schultz's choices may not have been seen as "smart business" at the time, but they were perfectly aligned with the company's greater vision, and the long-term results reflected that.

In a 2009 interview with CBS, Schultz said of Starbucks' mission, "We're not in the business of filling bellies; we're in the business of filling souls."

Howard Schultz's success story is just one example of how a strong vision that goes beyond short-term profit can create a company that inspires loyalty in its employees and customers alike.

Mindset and Company Vision

As your company's leader, you are the visionary of the business. Your desires, and your vision, will create an energy stream that trickles down to permeate every aspect of your business: every client, every employee, and every action taken within your company. Even if you're a solopreneur at the moment, or have just hired your first assistant, a strong, clear company vision is paramount to success.

Mindset plays a huge role in determining whether you can follow through with your company vision to achieve your goals around success, brand integrity, and expansion. It's all about what you believe is possible. According to "conventional" business wisdom, Howard Schultz's decision to expand health care and shut down thousands of stores for employee retraining should have tanked the company. Instead, it brought it back to life.

As they say, "Where there's a will, there's a way." Once

you decide what your vision, ideal client, and daily business operations need to look like in order for you to achieve your goals, don't compromise, and don't let "common knowledge" be your only barometer. Instead, commit to constant, consistent learning and growth. Work with your mentor or coach to get more clarity. Allow yourself to be "reprogrammed" for success on your own terms, and don't fall into the trap of catabolic energy. Remember, anabolic energy is both positive and limitless—and when you operate your company from that empowered place, everyone wins.

Your Avatar (aka, your ideal client)

As tempting as it can be to think that everyone in the world is a potential client, you can't serve everyone. If you try, you will quickly fall into the catabolic "money trumps all" mindset and dilute your company vision to the point where it no longer serves as a guidance system.

That's why your company vision should include an avatar—a model of your ideal client. Your company vision and values will speak directly to this person, and offer a perfect energetic match to their needs, desires, goals, and values.

When you know who you want to serve, and how this service will align with your company vision, you will have a much easier time developing products and services that will cater to your ideal clients and excite your audience.

Your ideal client (aka, your avatar) is the person you most want to serve, support, and uplift—the person you dreamed about working with when you created your business. You probably already know a lot about this person, but if you're not crystal clear about who they are and how you can help them, your company vision will be less targeted and less effective.

So, take the time to get to know your avatar. You can start by asking questions like these:

- Who is the person I most want to help?

- What are my avatar's biggest problems, and how will I solve them?

- What are my avatar's immediate concerns?

- What are my avatar's short-term goals?

- What are my avatar's long-term goals?

- What are my avatar's personal statistics? (For example: age, gender, income level, education level, location, interests, hobbies, habits, etc.)

- If your ideal client could only get one thing out of working with you, what would it be?

- When someone works with you, what will be their biggest takeaway?

- Aside from your actual services themselves, what qualities do you want your business to be known for (i.e., compassion, efficiency, deep knowledge) and how will you demonstrate those to your avatar through your services?

I know it seems like a lot of details, but when it comes to creating your avatar, you can never know too much. In fact, you want your ideal client avatar to be as real to you as your best friend. Why? Because when you get really specific about your audience and the work you want to do in the world, instead of talking to the room at large, you'll be talking to the person who really needs to hear what you have to say.

Once you know your avatar intimately, use your new knowledge to write your avatar, and the means by which you intend to serve him or her, into your company vision.

WORKING WITH YOUR TWO VISIONS

Now, it's time to merge your personal vision with your company vision, so that the two are able to operate in a complimentary way.

Your personal vision will always take precedence, because that's your vision for your whole life, not just for your work and wealth creation. If your company vision overshadows your personal vision, you will eventually start to slide into catabolic energy, overwhelm, and the destructive "small business" mindset we discussed in Chapter Two.

So, ask yourself the following questions:

- How does my company vision and overall goal parallel my personal vision?

- How do I want my business to support my overall vision for my life?

- Are there any places where my company vision contradicts or doesn't support my personal vision? If so, how can I adjust my company vision to complement my personal vision?

- Are there any places where I will need help implementing my company vision so that my personal vision isn't compromised?

If you find any discrepancies, adjust your company vision (including your ideal client avatar) so that it lines up perfectly with your personal vision. Then, write out final versions of your personal and company vision statements, and post them where you can see them both every day. That way, if one of them starts to slide, you'll notice and be able to correct it right away!

That said, neither your personal nor your company vision is set in stone. In fact, you'll want to revisit both of them weekly, monthly, and yearly. *You* are the visionary of your business; therefore, you need to review your vision, priorities, and goals anytime you are involved in a decision-making process. If anything doesn't feel aligned, it's time to change it.

In addition, your company vision should be reviewed with employees and subcontractors at least monthly, along with any additions to the vision such as new programs, services, and benefits. If your business mission or vision changes, your ideal client may change as well, so update your avatar at least every six months. If your business has shareholders, they should also review your company vision and avatar at least once a year. Allow your employees and shareholders to give feedback and make comments; this will let you know if you are sliding off-track and if anything needs to be adjusted.

Every entrepreneur's vision evolves over time. When my husband and I were married and running our small business, our vision could have been summed up in three phrases: "Survive. Pay bills. Work some more." It was very much a nose-to-the-grindstone mentality—not that we were aware of it at the time. Sure, we wanted to do better each year, but we didn't do any planning or discovery around our company and personal visions. We just got up and went to work each day, hoping for the best, trying to make as much profit as possible. What we wanted for ourselves, personally, got lost in the daily demands of the company. As I've shared, this created a draining catabolic energy spiral, and eventually led to our divorce.

When I started with Mary Kay Cosmetics, they had a

company vision. More, they had a protocol around how we, as consultants, would maintain that vision. It was the first time I had ever been introduced to that part of corporate culture. It opened up so many opportunities for me.

When I got into real estate investing, I applied what I'd learned in Mary Kay to my fledgling business. I asked myself, "How do I want my company to be seen in the community? What am I going to do for others?" It was a true test of developing my own identity and vision. I credit this visioning—and the planning I was able to do as a result—with my success in the real estate field, and my subsequent career as a speaker and trainer. My whole world changed because I went from simply ticking off my daily to-do list to creating something bigger than myself. At the same time as I was broadening my company vision, I was serving my personal vision by creating wealth and success on my own terms, and honoring my need for quiet time to work on my mindset and enjoy my life and relationships.

At each stage of my expansion, I took the time to revise my personal and company visions. My goals got bigger. My idea of success got blown wide open. My daily schedule evolved. Soon, I was living (and creating wealth) in realms I could never have imagined when I started out.

Your Offer: The Face of Your Vision

Your offers, products, and services are part of your company vision. Therefore, they should be totally aligned with the income you want to generate and with the needs and values of your avatar. Even more importantly, though, they must be aligned with your personal vision and your goals for work/life balance.

So, ask yourself: how do the things you want to accomplish with and for your clients intersect with the time you want to devote to your business? How much time will it take to deliver your offers or products with the level of integrity that your company vision demands? These are important things to know if you want to keep your visions, goals, and outcomes flowing toward your wealth attraction dreams.

For example, if your company vision for your coaching business is centered around helping clients create life-changing results, and your high-level offers are time-intensive programs like group and private coaching, you will need to put in a lot of hours to fulfill your company vision and make sure your offers are living up to their promises. This is great if your personal vision includes lots of work hours and personal energy. But what if your personal vision is to work only twenty hours per week, and create wealth through passive income streams? Suddenly, those one-on-one coaching hours, as lucrative as they may be, don't feel so aligned. In fact, they can quickly start to feel like drudgery.

Here's another example. Let's say that you're a real estate investor, and your company vision is to help people in stressful situations like divorce or job loss get out from under real estate that has become a burden. But because you've just started your business and are desperate for cash, you end up taking on projects that aren't aligned with your vision for helping others. You can then get caught in deals that stress you out and drain your energy, and end up with less bandwidth and capital to take on the projects that actually matter to you.

Any time there's a disconnect between your offers and your personal vision, it will affect your drive and desire, and ultimately your ability to attract wealth in your business. If you are too busy or stressed to be excited about what you're creating, your business will suffer. Period.

You'd be amazed how often I see these types of disconnections in my clients' businesses. Sometimes, they happen because the business is brand new, and the entrepreneur is trying any and all strategies to bring in clients. Sometimes, it's because the business has changed over time. And sometimes, it's because the entrepreneur's priorities have shifted but the company vision—including its key offers and avatar—hasn't followed suit. Regardless of the reasons behind them, these shifts always cause tension. A big part of my job is helping my clients reconcile these discrepancies and bring their business back into alignment with their visions before things spiral out of control or fall into a catabolic energy trap.

If you're noticing some gaps between what you're offering and what you really want to create, it's time to go back to the drawing board and create a strategy that will bring your offer back into alignment with your visions. Ask your mentor or coach for help, and make sure you're doing what you need to do to maintain a positive mindset. Remember, there is a solution for everything!

WHAT'S NEXT?

In this chapter, you've learned how to tap into the power of your vision to align your personal and business goals and take inspired action on the path to wealth.

Next, we'll look at a crucial aspect of success, and also one of the most difficult balancing acts in the entrepreneurial world: the place where you and your business overlap.

Yes, it's time to talk about your *expertise*.

CHAPTER FOUR

Your Expert Status

"The type of person you are is usually reflected in your business. To improve your business, first improve yourself."
- IDOWU KOYENIKAN

WHEN YOU WANT the best products, services, or advice, who do you call?

The experts, of course!

Whenever you make a major purchase, investment, or decision, you want to feel assured that you are receiving the best information, support, and value possible. Your ideal client feels the same way. That's why expert status in your field is so important to attain and maintain. You want to be that go-to resource on everyone's list.

HOW TO POSITION YOURSELF AS AN EXPERT

It has been asserted that, in order to gain true expertise in any field, you need to be actively engaged with it for 10,000 hours. This is true even of those who have exceptional inborn talent.

Truly successful people don't just have ability; they are willing to do whatever it takes to prepare themselves for success, including putting in those thousands of hours of practice. After all, some people have a knack for numbers, but no one is born knowing the ins and outs of investing!

If you are a new business owner (or even if you've been working in your business for a while), you might feel that, if you have to wait until you reach that magical 10,000-hour mark to call yourself an expert, you may as well throw in the towel right now. I'm here to tell you, don't give up! True mastery does, in fact, come from experience, but there's no reason why you can't make yourself a trusted resource for your clients and community long before you reach that tipping point.

You see, *expertise* is based on experience—but *expert status* is all about perception and mindset.

(Yes, we've circled back to mindset again. It truly is at the root of everything!)

As I mentioned above, you should always be learning and growing, both as a business owner and as a person. Expanding your knowledge in your field should be part of your daily to-do list. The more excited you are about accumulating knowledge, the faster you will move toward actually becoming an expert.

When I started my real estate business, I didn't just follow my mentor's instructions. I read everything about real estate investing and personal growth that I could get my hands on. I listened to audio books at the gym, in the shower, and in my car. I compared methodologies and opinions. I added new tips and tricks to my personal tool box. I still followed my mentor's method to the letter (because once you tweak a proven method, it's no longer proven), but the more I learned, the more I understood the *why* of what I was doing, and saw how all of the pieces fit together. Soon, I was able to navigate the world of real estate with far greater ease and confidence. I was walking the walk, not just talking the talk—and the more versed in my field I became, the more my clients' and peers' perceptions of me changed. I wasn't an "expert" yet, but the people who I wanted to serve regarded me as one, and my wealth and success expanded accordingly.

Attaining expert status in your field means becoming the go-to resource for your ideal clients, and achieving name recognition and brand association in your field. There are many ways to do that—but in order to really be successful with them, you have to walk your talk, speak to your niche, and continually grow your knowledge base. Otherwise, any gains you make will quickly be outpaced by changing markets.

I'll share more about specific ways to grow your audience in Chapter Six, but here are some simple things to consider as you begin to cultivate your expert status:

- *Find your niche.* Some people are afraid to niche because they think that they won't be able to find enough clients. But when you really narrow down your field of expertise, you can rise to the top more quickly. More, you can tailor your offerings to your ideal client, which results in greater success and results for everyone.

- *Educate your audience.* Share your knowledge through blogs, newsletters, speaking engagements, and any other opportunities you can create. Don't be afraid to "give away" what you know; the more useful information you can provide for people, the more they will value your expertise.

- *Get out there!* Network. Speak. Lead workshops. Meet people. Ask your existing clients for referrals. Name recognition is a big part of expert status, so don't hide out and wait for clients to come to you.

- *Treat yourself as the expert in your business.* Don't shortchange yourself by playing down the expertise you already have. You may not know everything yet, but own what you *do* know, and be willing to learn what you don't.

- *Invest in your growth.* Attend educational seminars and training events in your field. Join professional associations and online forums. Get around other like-minded people. The more you advance yourself in your field, the more quickly you will start thinking and acting like an expert.

- *Work with coaches and mentors.* This is another form of investing in yourself. A great coach or mentor will help to keep you accountable to your own development, both personally and in your business, and make sure you're not slipping into unhealthy patterns or catabolic energy.

- *Look at your circle of influence.* Are you surrounded by people who lift you up, or people pull you down? It's hard to believe in yourself as an expert if you're constantly bombarded with doubt and negativity. If someone in your circle isn't supporting your growth, try to create some space in that relationship so you can expand. Above all, don't let others' catabolic energy drag you down!

- *And, above all, walk your talk!* Congruency is a big deal. If I'm using my expert status to teach crowds of people about real estate investing, but I'm not currently investing or keeping up in my business, an energetic shift happens. Suddenly, I've moved from "do as I do" to "do as I say." Even if all of the right words are coming out of my mouth, there is an energetic disparity at play, and people can sense it. My sales plummet, and my audience's trust in me is lessened. But when I'm actively engaged in my own investments, the opposite is true. I'm walking my talk, people sense my authenticity, and my program sales skyrocket. It's a cycle I've observed over and over, and it holds true every time.

PLAYING THE PART OF THE EXPERT

If you don't act like an expert, you won't be seen as one.

This is true in every business, whether you're a coach or an investor, a writer or a restaurant owner. If you don't play the part of the expert in your business, you won't be perceived that way, no matter how many credentials you amass.

Expert status is more than just brand recognition; it's a state of mind. As the owner of your business, you are the visionary, the leader, and the driving force. You are the North Star by which everyone associated with your company—from employees, to clients, to peers and competitors—will navigate. Your energy sets the tone for your entire operation. This is why it's so important to make sure that you are always showing up in your life and business as the best possible version of yourself. In order to lead, you need to inspire others to follow.

So what does it mean to "act like an expert?" It's all about your mindset, and how you move through the world.

Do you set a positive example for everyone around you? Do you treat your employees and clients the way you'd want to be treated? Do you lead through promotion, and foster competition—or do you lead through inspiration and attraction?

Do you value your time and energy? As an expert, your time has value, so make sure you're setting clear boundaries around your schedule—especially when it comes to your personal time. If you want to gain, and preserve, a solid expert status, honoring your personal growth time is more important than fitting in one last client meeting before the weekend.

Are you presenting yourself as a consummate professional? Are you on time for meetings, both in-person and virtual? Are you prepared for your meetings (as much as humanly possible)? If not, arrange your schedule so that you have breathing room between your appointments, and make sure you're not rushing in and out. Minimize distractions (like phone alerts) as well.

Finally, are you speaking with honesty and integrity? Being an expert doesn't mean being all-knowing. Be willing to admit when you don't have the answer—but also be willing to find that answer, and follow up by whatever means necessary. This will not only increase your clients' trust in you, it will broaden your knowledge base and up-level your expertise at the same time!

Daily Mindset Hacks

In addition to conducting business with the highest possible integrity, there are other steps you can take every day to increase your expert status—and they may not be what you'd expect.

Your expert status starts with your mindset—which is greatly affected by the way you feel about yourself. If you don't have confidence in yourself, that lack of belief will undermine your positive attitude, sap your anabolic energy, and sabotage your business growth. Confidence comes in part with experience, but sometimes just showing up as though you were already at the top of your game can help give you the boost you need.

So, in addition to working on your mindset, thoughts, actions, and habits around your personal and business success, there are other simple things you can do to align your energy and mindset with your expert status and the wealth and success you want to create.

Mindset Hack #1: Take Care of Your Space

The energy of your home and work environment can strongly affect your mindset. Trust me, it's hard to feel successful if your space is dirty, cluttered, or chaotic. In fact, such an environment might even conjure thoughts of failure, and of being "not enough."

Is your house in order? Is it clean and organized? A cluttered or dirty home creates energy blocks that can affect your productivity, create added stress, and even impact your sleep! This factor doubles if you work from home.

Taking the time to clean up may feel taxing at first, but in the end it will improve your mindset and concentration, and help boost your gratitude for your space. (Even better, if your current budget allows, hire someone to clean for you. Several of my clients swear that a great cleaning service is one of the best business investments they've ever made!)

In that same vein, what is the condition of your vehicle? Is it clean, or does it resemble a rolling garbage can? Your car doesn't have to be a BMW or Mercedes—but you should care for it as if it is. That way, whenever you get in it, it will feel like a supportive space, not an embarrassment—and you won't go into meetings with little bits of yesterday's lunch stuck to your pants! More, when you take care of what you have—even if it's not what you ultimately hope to create—you establish a mindset of gratitude, and create positive new actions and habits around that mindset.

*Mindset Hack #2: Pay Attention to Your Appearance
and Presentation*

Are you presenting yourself to the world as a six- or seven-figure income earner? Are you dressed for success, with clothes pressed, nails groomed, and hair styled?

This isn't about impressing others (although when it comes to making business connections, it certainly doesn't hurt to look like a top earner). It's really about boosting your mindset and confidence. Presenting yourself as the best version of you—the version of you who lives the ideal life from your personal vision—will help to align you with your goals and attract people who compliment that vision. Remember, it all comes down to energy!

You don't have to spend a fortune to look your best, but a polished appearance does require a certain investment of time, so build your "prep" into your daily schedule. Designate time for hair, makeup, and cleaning/pressing your clothes every day, whether you have big meetings or not. Remember, you're showing up in the world as your successful self!

Here are some other ideas for up-leveling your personal presentation:

- *Personal tailoring.* Even inexpensive clothes can look flawless when they're tailored to your body. Invest in tailoring for key pieces like jackets, sport coats, dress pants, skirts, and formal shirts and blouses.

- *Clean your shoes.* It's an old rule, but it still holds true. Polished, clean shoes can make a huge difference in how you walk through the world.

- *Care for your hair.* Find a great stylist and visit him/her regularly. For big events, have your hair professionally styled.

Mindset Hack #3: Take Care of Your Body

Are you carrying extra weight or neglecting your physical health? If you're thinking negative thoughts about your body every time you look in the mirror—or worse, are dealing with pain or fatigue—you won't feel like an expert at the top of your business game.

If you're not in your best place physically right now, don't get on the self-blame train, because that never helps. Instead, start taking baby steps to shift your thoughts, actions, and habits around how you care for your body. Soon, you'll be feeling like your most energetic and confident self again.

Mindset Hack #4: Get Proper Rest

If I get less than seven hours of sleep, I start to get run down, stressed out, and overwhelmed. You probably have a "magic number" of sleep hours, too—so be sure you're getting the amount of rest that keeps you in your "sweet spot."

Mindset Hack #5: Just Show Up

When in doubt, suit up, show up, and do your best! That's Mindset 101 right there!

WHAT'S NEXT?

Now that you're clear on why your expert status is so vital to wealth attraction and the success of your business, it's time to move forward through inspired action. In the next chapter, we'll look at some specific ways to choose and execute action steps that are aligned with your personal and company visions, and which prioritize your expertise.

CHAPTER FIVE

Action

"Do it, and then you will feel motivated to do it."
- ZIG ZIGLAR

ACTION IS THE THIRD KEY to Accelerating Wealth. It's the bridge between your vision and your reality, and the only way to create what you really desire.

Action follows vision. Vision is the destination; action is what moves you toward that destination.

Inspired action stems directly from your personal and company visions, and propels you toward the fulfillment of those visions. It is always aligned with your mission, ethics, and greater purpose in the world, and never contradicts your values for the sake of expedience.

Sometimes, inspired action may appear to run counter to popular business wisdom, but—as we discovered in Howard Schultz's story in Chapter Three—it is always aligned with a greater goal. When you operate from anabolic energy and a positive mindset, you will recognize that a win for one is a win for all, and the outcomes you achieve will be more satisfying than just earning a paycheck.

HOW VISION INFLUENCES ACTION

There are two types of work that you will engage with as a business owner: work *in* your business, and work *on* your business.

The first kind of work is tied to the survival of your business. The second is tied to the growth of your business.

Chances are, there are a million practical things you need to do in your business every day to keep things running— things like fulfilling current projects or orders, bookkeeping, staff management, etc. These items are vital, but they're not the actions that will help you attract and create greater wealth. They will help you maintain the status quo, but they won't move you closer to your vision.

On the other hand, work *on* your business is the kind of work that fosters expansion. This is work like marketing, networking, and education, as well as the work you do to up-level your expert status and improve your mindset and energy. Above all, this work should be done with the highest possible mindset and energy, since it is the work which will shape your business's future, and help to create your personal and company visions.

Personal Vision Clarity Exercise

If you have a big vision but aren't sure what steps to take to get to where you want to go, try the exercise below. (Actually, everyone should do this exercise, even if they are already crystal clear!)

By charting a path backward from your ultimate goal to where you are now, you will be able to more easily identify the action steps, short-term goals, and stepping stones that link your current reality to the one you want to create.

The Personal Vision Clarity Exercise

- Find a quiet place to sit comfortably. Have a pen and paper within easy reach.

- Close your eyes. Take a few slow, deep breaths in and out to release the tension from your body.

- Now, envision, as you did in Chapter Two, where your ultimate success is, what it looks like, and what it feels like. Who is there with you? What are people saying? What does your typical day entail? Sit for a moment, immersed in your version of ultimate success. Use as many of your senses as you can, so you can actually *feel* it (as opposed to just intellectualizing it).

- Continue breathing while feeling the energy of your success settle completely in your body. Enjoy these feelings, and celebrate them.

- Now, consider how you got here to this place of ultimate success. See yourself taking action: What are you doing? Who are you speaking to? What are you saying? What is going on around you? One by one, trace your actions back to where you are right now, today. You have just charted a path to your ultimate success.

- Take a few deep breaths, and open your eyes. Grab your pen and paper, and write down all the action steps you envisioned yourself taking on the path to ultimate success. Don't let your ego get involved; instead, listen to your inner wisdom. See the chain of events as though it has already happened.

- Set goals around each of the action steps you identified. If the steps seem large or overwhelming, break them down into smaller steps that you can manage more easily.

- Now, assign timelines to your goals. Make them reasonable, so you don't sabotage your own success with unrealistic expectations—but don't space them too far apart, either. You want to create a sense of motion and progress.

THE AIM SMART PLAN

The goals we set around our personal and business visions can feel overwhelming, particularly if they require us to take sustained action or many smaller actions in order to reach them. Instead of giving up or falling into "survival mode," take the time to create a well-designed action plan that moves you forward every day.

One of my favorite blueprints for inspired action plans is the AIM SMART plan. This lovely acronym helps you break down any action plan into bite-sized chunks that you can implement with a minimum of stress. Create an AIM SMART plan for every major milestone you need to reach in order to achieve your vision.

The AIM SMART Plan

- *A* stands for the *acceptable minimum* you are willing to do toward completing this goal. The "A" in the AIM gets you started, and it is better than doing nothing.

- *I* represents your *ideal completion date* of this first step.

- **M** stands for what is the *middle* or a realistic "stretch goal" that you can reach within a set time frame. When setting the realistic stretch goal, again the key is to make it time-oriented, so as to provide you both a measurable checkpoint, and also to provide you a sense of accomplishment toward reaching your goal.

- **S** stands for the *specific step-by-step processes* on how you will reach your goal.

- **M** stands for *measurable checkpoints* (like your stretch goal) which assist you to quantify you have completed a specific step.

- **A** stands for *achievable steps* in the plan you are constructing.

- **R** stands for *reasonable expectations* that what you are saying you are going to be able to do can be done at the current time.

- **T** stands for *time*—as in the specific dates and times by which you will complete each step in the process.

PRIMING THE PUMP

Planning is a key part of wealth attraction—and it doesn't just apply to goal-setting. It also applies to the flow of your business, and the actions you take to work on your business.

When I teach the Wealth Attraction Formula to my clients, I talk a lot about "priming the pump." Imagine an old-fashioned hand pump, the kind that people used to draw water from wells before most homes had electricity. To get water to come out of the spigot, you needed to work the lever several times so the pressure would build up, drawing water out of the well.

Eventually, the water would come out—and when it did, it wouldn't come out in a trickle, but in a gush.

Taking action by working on your business is like priming that well pump. It may not seem to be creating results at first—but when it does, you will see not just a trickle of wealth, but a steady stream. If you keep working the pump, the wealth will keep flowing. This results in a constant flow of abundance.

The lesson here: *inconsistent action produces inconsistent results.*

Too many people stop working on their businesses before their "pump" is fully primed. They'll see a trickle of abundance, and stop working the pump. When the flow dries up, they start furiously pumping again—but only until they get another trickle. This cycle creates a lot of stress (aka, catabolic energy), and is not at all conducive to creating long-term wealth and success.

Part of your job as the visionary and expert in your business is to keep working that pump until you have a powerful stream of abundance gushing into your bucket. Then, you need to *keep going* so that the flow stays steady. Regardless of how well your business is doing right now, don't stop encouraging that flow! You can always grow your business to meet increasing demand (in fact, that's kind of the point) but you'll never sustain growth if you try to tap the well only at need.

DELEGATION: THE SECRET TO GROWTH THROUGH ACTION

M. Scott Peck wrote in *The Road Less Traveled: A New Psychology of Love, Traditional Values, and Spiritual Growth,* "Until you value yourself, you won't value your time. Until you value your time, you will not do anything with it."

What does this have to do with delegation? Everything!

Many business owners are afraid to delegate. There are two common reasons for this. First is a fear of spending money. Telling themselves that their business isn't "big" enough yet to hire help, they add more and more items to their to-do lists, hoping that someday they will feel wealthy enough to delegate.

The second reason for not delegating is directly tied to the deadly small business mindset. Many business owners think that no one can do things the way they do, and so they hoard all the tasks in their business until the overwhelm becomes too much to handle.

Both of these reasons for avoiding delegation are understandable, and even valid in some cases—but in the end, they're just excuses. Delegation is necessary if you want to create a business that produces real wealth.

You are the expert and visionary in your business. Therefore, your time should be spent on tasks that only a visionary and expert can accomplish. Every hour you invest in action that moves your business toward your vision will produce a measurable return—maybe not immediately, but down the road. But if you are too busy working in your business to work on your business, you will quickly find yourself in survival mode, where growth is impossible.

More, you should consider your personal vision and how delegation can feed it. If you are constantly struggling to keep up with mundane tasks that others could easily help with, you are probably not living your personal vision of work-life balance. This will quickly lead to frustration, disenchantment, and a catabolic energy spiral.

The good news is, delegation doesn't have to happen all at once. You can take baby steps toward freeing up your valuable time. When you take even a few basic tasks off your plate, I promise you will feel a surge of energy and inspiration. In fact, you'll wonder why it took you so long to do it!

Delegation Ideas

If you're not sure where to start with delegation, here are some ideas:

- *Make a list of tasks that you dread in your business.* Anytime you sit down to accomplish a task you dislike, you raise your catabolic energy level. You're no longer acting from an inspired place. You may even feel like a victim to your business. Maybe it's social media management that makes you grind your teeth. Maybe it's your monthly bookkeeping. Maybe it's cleaning your office. Whatever your most-loathed tasks are, ask yourself, "How can I assign this task to someone who actually enjoys it?"

- *Look for partners who are strong where you are weak.* Your expertise is the foundation of your business—but you can't be an expert at everything. Are you an action-taker? Look for someone who can help you manage the mundane details so things don't fall through the cracks. Feel hopeless when it comes to marketing? Hire someone who lives for the sale. You'll be able to devote your energy to the things that really light you up.

- *Look at income potential rather than the cost of delegation.* I have a client who charges $300 an hour for her coaching services. She used to spend 6-8 hours a month on bookkeeping and tax recording tasks— which, of course, was time she couldn't bill out for client work. When she looked at the numbers, she discovered that a professional bookkeeper could handle her tasks in 4 hours, at a cost of $50/hour ($200/month). By delegating, my client has freed up six or more potential income hours per month, which could net her $1,800.

- *Make a list of tasks that carry the highest wealth attraction potential for you.* Since you are the expert in your business, where is your time best spent? What tasks generate the most income and business growth for you? Where can you prime the pump? Now, come up with a plan to delegate at least three tasks that didn't make your list.

MORE INSPIRING WAYS TO WORK WITH ACTION

Your Priority To-Do List

I have a master to-do list that I update regularly. This list often has upward of 100 items on it. If I worked only from this list, I would feel completely overwhelmed, and would quickly burn myself out.

Instead, every night before I go to bed, I create a list of five high-priority items that must be accomplished the following day. I write these five "priority actions" on a separate sheet of paper, and place them on my desk so I will see them first thing in the morning. Then, when I wake up, I address these items right away. That way, no matter how the rest of my day goes, I know that I have accomplished the most pressing actions, and haven't dropped any balls.

I also make sure that at least one of my priority actions is related to my personal and business growth, and not just daily management. This way, I'm constantly taking steps to further my personal and business visions.

Your Calendar

My calendar is my life mapped out on screen. I schedule *everything*—from business meetings and travel time to exercise and personal care. If it's not on my calendar, it isn't getting done.

Successful wealth attractors know how to organize their time. They schedule every action step in their days—including those which further their personal visions. That way, they aren't tempted to overwork in unnecessary areas, or put off taking care of themselves.

Every action you need to take in your business, on your business, and for your own growth should be in your calendar. Once a week, sit down and add all of your appointments and commitments. Then, add time to execute any action steps related to your personal and business visions and your AIM SMART plans, as well as the hours you need for personal care and "prep time," exercise, self-development, and relaxation.

ACTION IN UNFORESEEN CIRCUMSTANCES

Sometimes, you can't plan for what happens in your business.

When the unforeseen occurs, your mindset really comes front and center. Successful people who operate from anabolic energy realize that we can't control what happens in our businesses; we can only control how we *respond* to what happens.

When you have a strong, positive mindset, you will naturally be less affected by the emotional roller-coaster of business ownership. You won't get caught up in worry when clients miss appointments, or when a coveted deal falls through. (This is especially true if you have taken the appropriate actions to "prime the pump.") A greater sense of equilibrium means that you will also be less likely to make important decisions from a place of victimhood, desperation, anger, or fear. Instead, you'll be able to look at the big picture, and treat whatever comes as a temporary setback.

So, when unforeseen circumstances come up, don't be tempted to slide into a negative mindset. Instead, use your personal development tools and practices to balance your energy. Then, tap into your inner wisdom and intuition to find the most inspired possible action to apply to the situation.

WHAT'S NEXT?

Wealth creation starts with desire and vision, but it hinges on action. In the next chapter, we'll talk about where action and your expert status overlap: in your marketing and sales.

Visibility is important to the success of any business, but if you're serious about creating wealth, it's even more crucial. When you stop playing small and really shift into a "big business" mindset, you'll step onto a bigger stage and start attracting even more of what you want for yourself and your company.

CHAPTER SIX

Wealth Attraction Marketing

*"Good marketing makes the company look smart.
Great marketing makes the customer feel smart."*
- JOE CHERNOV

WHEN YOU CREATED your vision for your business, you discovered your "avatar"—your ideal client, and established your role as the expert in your business. Now, it's time to go beyond vision and take action to bring your business to the people you want to serve more than any others.

Effective marketing in the Wealth Attraction Formula is less about specific techniques and strategies and more about authenticity, integrity, and alignment. Those factors empower you to create messaging that speaks directly to both your unique expertise and your ideal client.

Marketing falls into the "Action" step in the Five Keys to Accelerating Wealth, and as such is tied directly to your desire and vision. In this chapter, we'll explore some ways in which you can take action around marketing to move your personal and company visions forward, and take measurable steps toward creating the wealth and success you've been dreaming of.

MARKETING AND MINDSET

Maintaining a positive mindset is crucial to marketing success. In fact, it might be the single most important factor in your marketing strategy.

If you are caught in a catabolic energy loop, if you doubt your abilities to sell your products or compete in your market, or if you're operating from a belief that says, "If I want to win, someone else must lose," your marketing will be less effective. When this happens, you may be tempted to blame the marketing action itself, thinking things like, "This strategy will never work for me. I don't know why I even bothered." However, such defeatist thoughts only exacerbate the cycle of catabolic energy, stress, and lack mentality.

Of course, there will be marketing strategies which are more effective for your business and niche, and you may have to try several before you find your "sweet spot" for reaching your ideal audience. However, the energy you bring to your business can, and does, carry over into every interaction you have with clients and potential clients, even through your web site, social media, and other online forums. When you take the steps necessary to maintain and raise your personal energy level, you will naturally have greater success with *any* marketing strategy.

Marketing mindset can be tricky. Some of the most common fears associated with catabolic energy show up in the arena of marketing, because "putting yourself out there" is a great source of discomfort for many people. For example, a catabolic mindset might produce thoughts like these:

- I don't have money to spend on marketing right now.

- No one will care about my business since I'm small and just starting out.

- There's too much competition in my niche. I'll be just another face in the crowd.

- Sales just isn't my thing.

As I share with my clients, "You can't cheat your way to success, and you can't cheap your way to success." Marketing, especially when you are just starting out, is an investment in your business's future, not a quick-fix to get clients or stomp out your competition. Just like your expert status takes time and consistency to build, your marketing strategy, over time, will reinforce your brand's vision, aesthetic, and goals. This may require some initial investment, but in the end, a positive marketing mindset is about taking the long view, and not getting attached to immediate outcomes.

Remember, the Wealth Attraction Formula is about creating real success over the long term, not creating a boom month followed by a bust year. When you are focused only on getting your next client, and are caught in a do-or-die mind trap, you are more likely to make unwise, or even unethical, marketing choices. On the other hand, when you can keep your energy flow in an anabolic space, you are more likely to make smart marketing investments, appreciate the small wins, build a firm foundation for your business over time, and make decisions which enhance your brand and your vision in the long term.

MARKETING AND VISION

Marketing, like most other actions you will take in your business, is a direct outgrowth of your vision. In order to market effectively, you need to be tapped in to both your personal and company visions, and make strategic decisions about messaging, presence, and outreach which support those visions.

In the last chapter, you completed your Personal Vision Clarity Exercise, in which you worked backward from your ultimate goals to create a plan of action for your life and business. The results of this exercise—particularly the action steps you identified as stepping stones to your vision—will be crucial to your marketing strategies because they will show you where you need to focus your energy.

In order to create a vision-based marketing strategy, take some time to examine your overall action plan, and ask the following questions:

- What specific action steps did you identify which require you to create revenue and growth in your business?

- How much revenue/growth do you need to create in order to complete each step of your action plan?

- How many clients do you need to serve in order to create the amount of revenue above?

- What marketing avenues/strategies do you intend to explore in order to reach those clients (i.e. advertising, networking, social media, etc.)?

- How can you approach each of these marketing avenues/strategies in a way that feels aligned with your personal and company vision, your unique expertise, and your ideal client's personality and values?

You can start with a general strategy based on the questions above, and then refine it as you discover what works for you and your business. The important thing is that you don't feel like you are sacrificing your personal or company vision for the sake of your marketing. For example, if your dream is to create a global brand, you may still benefit from local networking (at least in the beginning), but you will want to put more energy into an online presence and/or physical travel in order to reach potential clients in various locations. On the other hand, if your dream is to create a go-to local business which serves your community, your online presence will still serve you, but you may see greater benefit from in-person networking through your neighborhood business associations.

As long as you conduct yourself with integrity (more about that later in this chapter), there is no right or wrong way to market your business. It's all about what works with your mindset, vision, and action plan.

NICHE MARKETING

When you created your vision and got in touch with your expert status, you probably identified—at least in some part—a niche market for your services or products. However, if you are still feeling a bit vague about your ideal client's needs and wants, you'll want to take the time to get to know your avatar before implementing any marketing strategies on a large scale.

As Meredith Hill said, "When you speak to everyone, you speak to no one."

There are plenty of potential customers out there for you. There are people who will resonate with your voice, your services, your products, and your vision more than they do with anyone else's. Chances are, these are people who are just like your avatar.

If you don't believe this—and I mean *truly* believe it—you may want to do some mindset work before you move forward. When you are stuck in scarcity mentality, thinking that there aren't enough clients for both you and your competition, or that not enough people need what you're offering, you will flow catabolic energy. You might even (subconsciously) sabotage the expert status and niche market you are trying to create. On the other hand, if you cultivate an anabolic energy flow and work from the belief that there is always enough to go around, you won't fear competition because you will automatically put yourself out there as the leader in your niche.

How do you create a niche marketing strategy that speaks to your ideal clients? One way is to ask your ideal clients what they think! What do they want from you? How do they want to receive the unique product or service that you are providing? Online surveys, Facebook polls, and e-mail inquiries are all effective ways to get actionable feedback. You can also talk with existing clients about why your services work so well for them. Most happy customers are thrilled to get a chance to provide in-depth feedback and share their experiences with you.

Experiential Marketing:
The Emotional Connection

Maya Angelou said, "I've learned that people will forget what you said, people will forget what you did, but people will never forget how you made them feel."

One of the most effective ways to market your business to your niche is to create an experience your ideal clients will never forget—an experience that will keep them talking about you, your brand, and your expertise for weeks and months to come.

No matter how brilliant your marketing strategies, nothing beats good, old-fashioned word of mouth. "Social proof" is the most powerful form of marketing you can employ, and the more in tune with your niche you are, the more word of mouth will benefit your business.

This may sound daunting, but the details of how to do this are already written out for you in your personal and company visions. You can create emotion-driven experiences based on the ways in which you dream of serving your ideal clients and the results you want to help them achieve.

For example, I co-lead a high-level mastermind group for entrepreneurs. Because our focus is on helping our members create thriving businesses and top-notch lifestyles, we choose to hold our live events at the best hotels in the country. Participants benefit from thoughtful details like signature leather binders (rather than cheap paper ones), beautiful branded writing implements, delicious food, and plenty of time to indulge in luxurious amenities.

Could we hold our events in moderately-priced hotel conference rooms? Of course. But the energy of a mediocre venue wouldn't match our brand or vision, nor would it evoke the emotions associated with top-level success for our participants. In fact, trying to match our exclusive brand with a modest location would actually create a misalignment in our marketing. After all, how can you call yourself a 5-star company when you're only serving up a 3-star experience?

Creating memorable and emotionally-driven experiences demands extra time and resources, but the effort is well worth it, no matter what demographic you're serving. Remember, what your clients will remember most is how you make them *feel*.

When you have a happy client who feels good to be a part of what you're creating, and that happy client shares their experience with someone in their inner circle—someone who shares their values, interests, and struggles—you are almost guaranteed to gain from that referral. The return might not be immediate, but the more buzz and emotional connection you create, the more likely you are to be the first person on those potential clients' call lists.

DOS AND DON'TS OF WEALTH ATTRACTION MARKETING

As I mentioned previously, marketing for Wealth Attraction isn't so much about a specific marketing plan as it is about an *energetic marketing strategy*. In other words, you need to start with the right mindset, flow it through your company vision, create an emotional bond with your ideal, niched clients, and align your actions with not only your desire for wealth but also with your personal and company integrity.

There are a million ways to physically go about the task of marketing your business. Chances are you have a few in the works already. Any and all of them can work, as long as they complement the energy flow you are creating, and feel aligned to you both personally and professionally.

You are the poster child for your brand, so you need to walk your talk—especially in your marketing, since that is the first contact most of your potential clients will have with you and your company. For example, if your core message is about empowering people, hard-sell strategies that force potential clients into corners are not going to be aligned with your vision or your products.

With so many ways to create visibility in today's marketplace, you will probably run into some gray areas—marketing strategies that seem like a great idea but still feel just a little bit "iffy." Thankfully, determining whether a particular strategy is aligned with your energy and vision is easier than you think. Just take some deep breaths, close your eyes, and ask yourself how it feels in your body. Does it feel open and expansive, like an invitation—or "sticky" and aggressive, like a hard shove? If it's the latter, it might be because you're taking a strategy that's out of integrity.

Of course, there are some marketing choices which (in my opinion) will always be misaligned, and tied to catabolic energy and an unhelpful scarcity mindset. That's why I created my Dos and Don'ts for Wealth Attraction Marketing. These are general guidelines for everyone who wants to market their business in an aligned way, regardless of niche or specialty.

Dos And Don'ts For Wealth Attraction Marketing

- ***DON'T guess at what your ideal clients want or need.*** When you created your avatar, you got as clear as humanly possible about your ideal client and how you want to serve him or her. However, don't assume that, just because you know who your avatar is, you also know what he or she wants and needs, or think that it's up to you to create a need where one doesn't exist. There is no substitute for actual feedback, so ***DO reach out through e-mail and/or Facebook polls, surveys, and other avenues*** to discover how you can provide the answers your ideal clients need.

- ***DON'T shove your business card in the face of everyone you meet,*** especially when you're not in a networking venue. If you're involved in a multi-level marketing (MLM) company (or have been in the past), you may be getting advice that says, "Stick a business card in the face of anyone within a three-foot radius." However, this is a big turnoff for most people, particularly in the upper echelons of the business world. Instead, ***DO take the time to get to know the people you're meeting.*** If they truly are your ideal clients, the opportunity to speak about what you offer will come naturally. It's far better to have two fruitful conversations in an evening than give out two hundred business cards that yield no sales.

- **DON'T sell or network at inappropriate times.** When I teach investment workshops for my mentor, Robert Kiyosaki, we have strict rules about networking. Since Robert pays to put on these multi-day events, we ask that our participants refrain from selling their own services until our specified networking time at the close of the workshop. This encourages an atmosphere of respect, both for us as the producers of the event and for the other professionals attending. Put another way: don't go into other people's venues to sell your stuff! Instead, **DO join professional associations, membership organizations, and networking groups** that also attract your ideal clients.

- **DON'T act like an amateur, or speak disrespectfully about your competitors.** This rule ties into #2 and #3, but it also applies to every interaction you have, both in person and online. Be authentic, but don't air your dirty laundry. Ask for feedback, but don't criticize what others in your field are doing. **You are the face of your business and the expert behind your brand, so DO be sure to present yourself that way,** whether you're at a multi-million-dollar event or posting on your personal Facebook page. Respect other people and what they are doing, and they will respect you in turn.

- ***DON'T send mixed messages.*** I meet a lot of people who have one face for their professional lives, and another for their personal lives. Which one is real? Should your customers trust the "you" who shows up on your website, or the "you" on your personal Facebook page or Instagram account? Don't fool yourself into thinking that people can't see through your business persona. To avoid losing your clients' trust, ***DO be sure you're walking your talk, even when you're off the clock.***

WHAT'S NEXT?

Now that you've moved through the first three Keys to Accelerating Wealth—Desire, Vision, and Action—it's time to move on to Key number four, Accountability. In the next chapter, we'll talk about how accountability to yourself, your vision, your clients, and your mentors can help you stay on the fast track to success and the fulfillment of your dreams!

CHAPTER SEVEN

Accountability

"Accountability breeds response-ability."
- STEPHEN R. COVEY

ONCE YOU HAVE ESTABLISHED your vision, created your action plan, and started putting yourself out there as an expert in your field, you will be in a flow. You'll probably be feeling like you are gaining momentum and traction, and like you are starting to see real progress toward both your company and personal visions.

In other words, you're packed up and ready to go on your journey to wealth and fulfillment!

It's true that it's easier to keep momentum going once you've begun something. But, as many entrepreneurs discover, the highway to wealth creation is littered with cross-streets, neon signs, and a million other potential distractions. If you don't keep your eyes on the road, you can quickly lose sight of where you're going, take a wrong turn, and end up somewhere you never anticipated.

This is why it's vital to establish *accountability* to both your personal and company visions. When you have guideposts in place, you are far less likely to get lost, distracted, or turned around. Accountability is more than just a sense of responsibility; it's a system you create in order to fulfill your responsibilities in the most aligned and forward-moving way possible.

Accountability, in the Wealth Attraction Formula, takes place on multiple levels:

- Accountability to your personal vision
- Accountability to your company vision
- Accountability to your clients/customers
- Accountability to your mentors and coaches

In this chapter, we'll talk about each of these types of accountability, and how you can create a structure to support your growth, positive mindset, and overall success.

Why Is Accountability So Important?

If there's one thing I've learned after decades of observing people in multiple areas of life and business, it's that *success without integrity doesn't last*. Eventually, misalignments show through even the shiniest veneer. If you want to create lasting wealth, fulfillment, and success, integrity in all things should be at the top of your priority list.

Being in integrity isn't just about being authentic, as we discussed in Chapter Six (although authenticity is a big part of it), but also being true to your word—doing what you say you are going to do, in the way you say you are going to do it. It's about walking your talk. It's about being the face of your brand, and living up to the standards you set for both your personal and company vision.

The trouble is, sometimes, when we're deep in the daily grind, it's hard to see where we are slipping out of alignment. I see this most often when it comes to my clients' personal visions. They are so focused on over-delivering for their clients and building their companies that they lose sight of why they started down this path in the first place. They make choices with their time and energy that don't support their personal visions of freedom and expansiveness. They sacrifice their personal dreams in favor of growing their revenue. This works for a while, but inevitably they start to feel trapped by their businesses, or even hate the work they once loved.

When you have an accountability system in place, the small detours away from the path to your vision don't become full-on U-turns. You are able to course-correct much more effectively and efficiently because you have people on your team who can gently redirect you when you've lost sight of why you're really doing what you're doing, and who can help you do what you need to do to get there.

ACCOUNTABILITY TO YOUR PERSONAL VISION

Your personal vision is your guiding light. It's your North Star, the beacon by which you navigate all of the various facets of your life. It is your highest priority, and the ultimate deciding factor for every action you take.

And yet, somehow, personal vision ends up taking a backseat for many people. Instead of treating it as their North Star, they regard their vision as more of a treasure map—a fun fantasy to be dragged out when things ease up and they have some breathing room, but not anything on which to base daily strategy and business decisions.

This is backwards thinking. If you don't have a strong personal vision to guide you, you will end up working yourself in circles. You won't find the fulfillment you dream of, or create a lifestyle of freedom and joy, because you won't even know how or where these things exist for you. You might make some money, but will you be truly wealthy? Probably not.

In the Wealth Attraction Formula, personal vision trumps all. Your company vision can change. Your ideal client can evolve. You can move on from coaches and mentors who no longer stimulate your growth. But if you want to create real wealth on your own terms, your personal vision must be central to every action you take.

How do you stay accountable to your personal vision? The key lies in your vision itself. Look at what you want to create, and start creating it—even if you can only manage a little piece at a time right now. If you want to create a spacious lifestyle, don't allow yourself to become a slave to your work; instead, even when things are hectic, make time every day to just be. If you want to align with material wealth, surround yourself with wealthy energy whenever possible. If you want to be happy, calm, and open, engage in personal growth practices that support those feelings. Ask yourself what you truly want, and then find ways to bring that energy into your daily life, no matter what else is going on.

Every other month or so, I take time to travel to an exclusive luxury location for a solitary mini-retreat. I book a room in a beautiful hotel, and spend a couple of days enjoying the high-end restaurants, shopping, and just immersing myself in the energy of one of the nation's wealthiest communities. During this time, I examine my short- and long-term goals, plan out my action steps for the next few days, weeks, and months, and generally check in with myself and my personal vision to make sure I'm still on the right track. This time is vital for me in staying accountable to my vision for a wealthy, healthy, happy life. It's an energetic reset, and part of the way in which I walk my talk as a wealthy, successful person.

To me, being in an environment where I'm surrounded by the trappings of wealth helps me align with wealth energy. It's part of the way I walk my talk; by investing in myself in a way that makes me feel pampered and valuable, I reinforce the mindset that I am abundant, and worthy of abundance. Could I create the same alignment if I chose to save money and stay in a Motel 6? I doubt it. That, to me, would be incongruent with my personal vision and incompatible with my wealthy mindset. I would essentially be saying to myself, "I want to be wealthy, but I don't believe that I have enough to move through the world like a wealthy person."

Of course, I'm further along in my wealth journey than many people. For those who are just starting their Wealth Attraction journey, creating accountability through experience will (and should) look a bit different. After all, putting on a "rich" façade while struggling to pay your bills will create just as much energetic incongruence as a scarcity mindset!

The best and easiest way to stay accountable to your personal vision is to keep your vision at the forefront of your mind at all times. Post your personal vision statement on your office wall. Hang your vision board in a place where you can see it multiple times per day. Carve out small chunks of time each week to take actions that move you closer to your personal and lifestyle goals and provide you with inspiration—whether that's walking in the woods, going out on the town, working out, meditating, or snuggling up with a great book.

As your company grows and your wealth increases, your personal vision can and should evolve. However, when you do make a change to your personal vision, be sure it's for the right reasons, and not as a concession to the demands of your business or some other change in your life.

You will know when it's time for your personal vision to shift when it no longer excites and motivates you. Maybe you've outgrown some of your old dreams. Or, maybe you've reached the goals you originally set around your wealthy, successful lifestyle, and it's time to expand even further. Maybe catabolic energy is surfacing, and you find yourself making excuses as to why you can't or shouldn't do the things on your list. Maybe you simply don't want what you thought you wanted. The reasons matter less than the underlying mindset and energy.

Above all, a wealthy life is a life that feels happy, fulfilled, abundant, and spacious. What those things mean to you, personally, form the foundation of your desires, which underpin your vision and action. Accountability to your personal vision, in the end, is accountability to what you want out of life. After all, you can start another business, or find another niche, but you can't start another life!

ACCOUNTABILITY TO YOUR COMPANY VISION

As an entrepreneur, your company vision is inextricably tied to your personal vision. Therefore, it will shift and change as your personal vision evolves. Ideally, when you're supporting one, you're supporting the other.

Being accountable to your company vision means doing whatever it takes to live up to the bar you've set for your company's success, growth, and service to your niche. It means walking your talk on the big stage, and making choices that are aligned with not only profit, but with your greater goals for service.

The number one way I stay accountable to my company vision is by continually learning and growing as an expert in my field. In order to do my best work and stay in an anabolic energy space, I need to be around like-minded people who are operating at my level. I pay for high-end masterminds and trainings, and go to conventions, trainings, and workshops several times per year. These aren't frivolous expenses or luxuries, but investments in my business.

If you're an entrepreneur alone at home, doing what you have to do to keep your business growing, you're probably not on a learning curve. If your company vision includes expanding beyond your spare bedroom, you've got to get out there and start connecting with like-minded people who can expand your thinking, challenge your notions of what's possible, and share new avenues for creating growth. I always encourage my high-level clients to go to conferences and spend time around people who are succeeding in their fields. Inevitably, they come back energized and brimming with new ideas.

The moment you stop learning and growing is the moment your company stops growing. Remember, your company vision supports your personal vision, so if you want to create and attract wealth in your personal life, you need to create and attract wealth in your business, too. Start by setting some goals around learning, education, and professional connection for the next six months, and then follow through with them. The more you dive into a space of growth, the more excited you will be to keep growing!

ACCOUNTABILITY TO YOUR CLIENTS & INVESTORS

How and why you serve your clients is a big part of your company vision. Therefore, accountability to your clients is central to alignment with your overall business vision and plan.

Being accountable to your clients encompasses more than just the obvious stuff like meeting deadlines, providing consistent quality in your services and products, and following up on compliments and complaints. Accountability in this sense is also about creating an atmosphere of open communication, authenticity, and transparency, and going above and beyond to create an *experience* for your clients that keeps them coming back for more.

Maybe it's just my old-fashioned business ethics at work, but I always encourage my clients to over-deliver for their customers. Remember, it's all about the way you make people feel. When your clients feel heard, valued, and appreciated, they are much more likely to recommend you to others in their community.

The same philosophy applies to your investors (if you have them). When I started my real estate business, I was able to attract many high-level investors even as a "newbie" because I consistently over-delivered. My investors saw faster returns at a higher rate because I made serving them a priority. They told their friends, and soon I had a line of investors knocking at my door to help me grow my business and create more wealth for everyone.

Of course, when you don't start from a positive mindset around over-delivery, it's all too easy to slip into a negative mindset of codependency, victimhood, or self-sacrifice. Once again, it all comes back to your personal vision, which is non-negotiable. Above all, you need to honor and prioritize your personal growth, goals, vision, and time. Set strong boundaries around your time, and don't over-commit yourself. This will keep your mindset and energy in alignment so you don't slip into burnout or a catabolic energy spiral, while ensuring you have the time and resources to keep your clients and investors 100 percent satisfied.

ACCOUNTABILITY TO YOUR COACH AND/OR MENTOR

Coaches and mentors play a huge role in keeping you moving toward your personal and company visions and goals. Therefore, practicing accountability to them really means practicing accountability to yourself and your business.

Ideally, you will have access to a coach, a mentor, or both from the time you start your business. That way, you are able to follow in the footsteps of someone who has done it before you, and receive advice and feedback that will keep you from making common mistakes or wandering off the path to your vision.

Coaches and mentors function in different capacities; therefore, your accountability to each will look and feel different. However, the end result—your growth, expansion, and wealth creation—is the same.

Accountability to Your Coach

A great coach is someone who can help you move toward your vision in an aligned way. You can also work with your coach to create action plans around your goals, and set up checkpoints and mile markers to keep you moving forward.

Not all coaches are created equal. When searching for a coach, look for someone who understands and resonates with the life and wealth you want to create, who is walking their talk, and whose methods feel integrous and positive to you.

Note that "integrous" and "positive" do not always equal "comfortable."

Accountability to your coach starts with your willingness to create and maintain a channel of transparency, integrity, and honest communication. When you start making excuses, deflecting, or slipping into catabolic energies like blame, fear, or scarcity, a good coach will always call you out.

As I often share with my clients, "You can make money, or you can make excuses, but you can't do both." Usually, when you run into fears or start making excuses, you are experiencing a mental or emotional block. Hearing that you are acting like a victim or sabotaging yourself through a negative mindset might not be the easiest thing in the world, but you need to be able and willing to receive such challenging feedback and take responsibility for your actions if you want to grow as a person and business owner.

A great coach will ask probing questions to pull out the real reasons for your resistance, but will never shame or belittle you. If you find that your mindset or energy plummets after a coaching session, it's time to find a new coach!

Accountability to Your Mentor

Working with a mentor is different than working with a coach. As we discussed in Chapter Two, a mentor is someone who has done what you want to do and is living the life you want to create.

Accountability to a mentor is less about rooting out problems than about reaching markers and milestones. Your mentor will give you advice and a process to follow, and it's up to you to do what you need to do in terms of planning, mindset, and action, to make it happen. Your mentor may have some insights into how to deal with fears or emotional blocks, but unlike a coach, rooting out those issues isn't in his or her job description.

Your mentor is the person whose tracks you can follow in the direction of your personal vision. So pay close attention to what your mentor does and says, and how he or she lives life. Ask about goal-setting and techniques for following through. If you've found your mentor through an educational program or system, chances are he or she will have ample material to share in this regard. Make sure you are following instructions to the best of your ability, and meeting the deadlines you and your mentor agree on.

IT'S ALL ABOUT INSPIRATION

Whatever accountability processes you set up, the end result should be that you feel inspired, motivated, and supported. Growing yourself and your business, and using that growth to create wealth, isn't always easy—but it shouldn't feel like an uphill battle all the time, either.

As with all of the Keys to Accelerating Wealth, a positive mindset and underlying anabolic energy flow are essential to creating and maintaining accountability to your personal vision, company vision, clients, coaches, and mentors. When in doubt, go back to the mindset basics we learned in Chapter One. Look at your circle of influence, your personal growth practices, your Wealth Attraction Factor, and any unhelpful beliefs you are still carrying about wealth, money, and success. When you run into a wall, it's usually because something big is shifting in your life—so lean into what's happening, get curious, and call on your coaches, mentors, and other resources for guidance. Soon, you'll have what you need to move forward and into the next phase of your Wealth Attraction journey!

WHAT'S NEXT?

Now that we've explored how to create and sustain your desire, vision, and actions through accountability practices, it's time to move on to the fifth Key to Accelerating Wealth: Celebration! This step will help you complete the cycle of manifestation, and motivate you to keep building on the wealth you've already created. Plus, it's a fun way to acknowledge all of the work you've done to set yourself up for ultimate Wealth Attraction!

CHAPTER EIGHT

Celebration: The Secret Ingredient

*"The more you praise and celebrate your life,
the more there is in life to celebrate."*
- OPRAH WINFREY

CELEBRATION IS THE FIFTH and final Key to Accelerating Wealth in the Wealth Attraction Formula. At first glance, it may seem incongruent with the other Keys, because it's not about forward motion, planning, or execution.

This step in the process gets ignored by a lot of would-be wealth creators. However, celebration isn't an "extra," or a "bonus." It's a full-fledged Key for good reason.

When you celebrate something, you pause to appreciate it. You honor it. You see it for what it is—and, most importantly, you give it *significance*.

On the other hand, when you don't celebrate something, you don't give it significance. You simply blow by it on the road to the next big thing. In fact, the less you acknowledge something, the less important it seems.

But if your successes—big or small—aren't important, what is?

In the end, as with everything else in the Wealth Attraction Formula, it all comes down to mindset. This final step in the

Wealth Attraction Formula is about creating a positive energy loop, and reinforcing that positivity with every step you take in the direction of your personal vision. I can't overstate the importance of this to your success, your personal energy, and your creation of true, lasting wealth.

THE DOWNSIDE OF MINIMIZATION

Have you ever felt that, no matter how hard you work, it never feels like enough?

If so, it's probably because you're minimizing your achievements.

As I mentioned when I introduced this Key in Chapter Two, those of us who are driven, motivated goal-setters tend to blow past milestones and forget our wins the moment they happen, since we're already on our way to bigger and better things. However, when we choose not to celebrate our accomplishments, we send a subtle (or maybe not-so-subtle) message to ourselves: what we have done *is not enough*, and we haven't won "big" enough to warrant acknowledgment from ourselves and others.

Think about that statement for a moment. It doesn't feel very good, does it?

Consciously, we may not see our minimizing behaviors in this way. Our minds may simply be leaping ahead to the next action step, the next goal, the next piece of our personal vision, and relegating the immediate past to the "less important" folder. It's understandable: as we meet milestones and look out over new horizons, our goals change, and get bigger. Our personal vision of what's possible expands. We're looking forward, not backward. But in terms of energy and subconscious mindset, this lack of acknowledgment sends a powerful message—one that can trigger a steep slide into catabolic energy. It says, "I am always three steps behind, running to catch up to what I know is possible."

Your personal vision is unique, but chances are (since you're reading this book) that exponential growth and wealth creation are central factors in it. You're here because you want to create massive expansion, both physically and mentally. But such expansion needs to be accomplished in stages, with attention to rejuvenation after a big growth spurt. Every time you reach a milestone, you need time to take a breath, realign your mindset and energy, establish a new baseline, and prepare for the next stage of the journey.

Think about it this way: if you were an athlete training for a triathlon, you wouldn't complete the whole course every single day for a month, go through the big event, and then do another triathlon the next day. You'd be exhausted, and might even do permanent damage to your body! Instead, you would start training in small pieces—running one day, swimming the next—and build up to the full course. Then, once the competition was over, you would rest for a week or so to let your body recover and realign before you moved on to the next challenge. More, you would congratulate yourself, and say things like, "Wow! I just did a triathlon!"

Business is no different. Celebrating your wins is your way to recuperate after the big race, and get yourself realigned so you can take on the next challenge from a nourished, positive place. When you minimize your wins, it's like saying, "I ran a marathon. So what? It wasn't an *ultramarathon*."

So please, stop minimizing your wins. Instead, pause, reflect, and celebrate. This will raise your anabolic energy, center you in your greater vision, and remind you of why you are doing this work in the first place.

Celebration Helps You Manifest More of What You Want

Celebration isn't just about getting centered and prepping for the next stage of the race. It's also about aligning your energy with your personal vision and what you want to manifest.

How you do this will depend on the type of personal growth work you've been engaged with. I personally believe that the entire universe is energy, and that we get back what we put out. This is why I always take the time to acknowledge and celebrate what I've achieved, even when my mind is already bouncing ahead to the next big project.

The Universe is attuned to, and responds to, our personal vibration. So when we feel gratitude and celebrate what we have achieved, we essentially tell the universe, "I want more of this, please!"

Put another way, celebration is like saying "thank you" to a friend who got you the gift for which you've been yearning. You wouldn't snatch such a present out of your friend's hands, set it aside, and ask, "What's next?" That would not only be rude, it would tell your friend in no uncertain terms that the gift wasn't good enough to merit your full gratitude and attention.

When you extend the same gratitude to the Universe (or the deity/energy of your choice) as you do to your friends, you will cultivate a constant vibration of gratitude, appreciation, and love. This will raise your overall vibration, elevate your anabolic energy, and bring you closer to the vision you hold for your ideal life. You will literally tune yourself in to the universal channel of "Yes! Thank you! I'll have more of that!"

I promise, this isn't woo-woo nonsense. It's real, and it works. Why? Because even more than extending gratitude to some unseen force, celebration as a Key to Wealth Attraction helps change the way you relate to success *within yourself.*

I've seen so many people create massive wealth and completely fail to enjoy it. They started off saying something like, "I want a beautiful home for me and my family." Then, when they made enough money to buy the home, they wanted the mansion. Then, they wanted the yacht. There's always something bigger and better on the horizon.

There's nothing wrong with having a yacht, believe me—but what's the point of having it when you don't take the time to celebrate and enjoy it?

When we don't stop to celebrate, feel gratitude, and raise our energy and mindset, we can lose track of why we are working so hard in the first place. We won't enjoy the material comforts that were such a big part of our vision. In fact, we can get so caught up in the *work* of creating our vision that the vision itself becomes secondary, and eventually starts to feel like a burden instead. When this happens, our optimism will inevitably nosedive into bitterness (aka, catabolic energy).

Real wealth isn't just about money and stuff. It's about your personal vision for a wealthy, fulfilled life, whatever that looks like. Action is about creating that life; celebration is about living it.

HOW TO CELEBRATE

When you think about "celebrating your wins," what comes to mind? How do you treat yourself when you've accomplished something really great?

If your answer is, "I don't know," you're not alone. I know so many entrepreneurs who think that the only reward they can or should claim for their efforts is the measurable growth of their business. But since you are more than just your business—

remember, your business exists to support your personal vision, not the other way around!—celebrating only in or for your business is limiting, and can easily lead to burnout.

So, spend some time thinking about what feels "celebratory" to you. What do you love to do but don't get to do very often? When you are celebrating other occasions (like birthdays, anniversaries, etc.) what festivities do you plan? And, most importantly, what actions create the feeling of being aligned with your greater personal vision? Your answers to these questions will provide clues as to how to celebrate your Wealth Attraction wins.

Celebrating your wins doesn't have to be flamboyant or expensive—in fact, if your current goals include getting out of debt or otherwise getting a handle on your finances, costly celebrations might actually set you back and trigger a catabolic energy cycle. It's all about what creates a vibration of gratitude for you, helps you tap into that expansive anabolic energy, and acknowledges what you have accomplished as a direct result of your positive mindset, desire, vision, action, and accountability.

Ideas for Celebrating Your Wins

- Take a hot bath with candles and essential oils, or a long, hot shower. Focus on how amazing you feel about your recent accomplishments.

- Get together with friends and toast one another's accomplishments.

- Take yourself out for tea, coffee, or a meal as a treat.

- Go on a yoga, spa, golf, or adventure retreat.

- Call your mentor or coach to gush about your win.

- Book your dream vacation.

- Open that nice bottle of wine you've been saving for a "special occasion."

- Make a list of your successes. Post it where you can see it every day.

- Share your accomplishments with your mentor or mastermind group.

- Take a whole day off!

Celebration can happen alone or with others. It can be simple or lavish. Again, it doesn't matter, as long as it makes you feel expansive, grateful, and nourished. However you choose to acknowledge your wins, though, make sure you do it regularly. ("Regularly" could mean monthly, weekly, or even daily.) This will support your anabolic energy and positive mindset, and keep you connected to your "why" for creating wealth and success.

WHAT'S NEXT?

You now have all the pieces of the Wealth Attraction Formula. You understand how to harness the power of desire to create your personal and company visions, how to use your vision to create concrete and achievable action steps, how to show up as an expert in your business, how to market and network effectively and with integrity, how to keep yourself accountable to your visions at all levels, and how to use celebration to cement your accomplishments and keep your mindset and energy elevated.

In short, you're already a rock star.

I'm living proof that nothing is out of your reach, if you are willing to learn and grow. I know that if you follow this process carefully, and work continuously on your mindset and personal growth, you will soon begin to see the wealth, success, and fulfillment you have been dreaming of!

Ann Sanfelippo
WEALTH ATTRACTION™
Academy

MANIFESTING THE LIFE OF YOUR DREAMS

How many times have you thought to yourself, "This is it! This is the year I am going to make all of my dreams come true," only to see that enthusiasm fade, sabotaged by your usual routine and the demands of daily living?

FIND A NEW PATH TO WEALTH & HAPPINESS

The Wealth Attraction™ Academy has developed a process you can follow that makes accomplishing all your goals a reality!

We help individuals build wealth while experiencing more joy and fulfillment. Founded in the Law of Attraction, my proven system will enable you to create a life by design—a life that opens opportunities to work less, create more money, and show up in the world as the best version of *you*, every day.

If you're interested in discovering how my Wealth Attraction Academy programs can help you build your business, attract wealth, and manifest the life of your dreams, please visit WealthAttractionAcademy.com to learn more. Be sure to register to receive your FREE "Attract Wealth, Health, & Happiness" 4-piece Gift Set!

CONNECT
WITH ANN

The Wealth Attraction™ Academy

WealthAttractionAcademy.com

Social Media

Facebook
Facebook.com/WealthAttractionAcademy

LinkedIn
LinkedIn.com/in/Ann-Sanfelippo-867124a

Twitter
@thewaacademy

HIRE ANN
TO SPEAK

ANN SANFELIPPO has been a high-demand, world-class keynote speaker for over a decade. She has spoken on over 500 stages and has built a reputation for speaking to the needs of busy professionals, entrepreneurs, and small business owners who desire to move beyond the traditional "hours for dollars" income model. Ann brings an irresistible energy and authentic presence to each talk she gives, encouraging and empowering her audiences to begin the transformational process for attracting wealth and creating success in business and life.

INVITE ANN TO SPEAK AT YOUR CONFERENCE OR EVENT

Speaking topics include wealth building, sales strategies, and leadership techniques, and can be tailored to both entrepreneurial and corporate audiences. To learn more, please inquire at **WealthAttractionAcademy.com/contact**.

ABOUT THE AUTHOR

ANN SANFELIPPO is the creator of the Wealth Attraction™ Academy. An international best-selling author, speaker, and coach, she guides entrepreneurs to accelerate wealth, health, and happiness through cultivating a positive mindset, harnessing the power of vision, and taking inspired action to propel them to success in their chosen fields.

Over the last two decades, Ann has "walked the walk" of a wildly successful entrepreneur, and has had the privilege to study successful influencers and business practices on an intimate level while building her own seven-figure business empire. After rising to top sales director for Mary Kay Cosmetics Sales Director, she created a huge real estate investment portfolio which allowed her to diversify into several new businesses and asset classes. She was so successful at this that she was approached to be a lead speaker/trainer for Robert Kiyosaki's Rich Dad Education brand, whose methods she employed in her own real estate business.

Ann is an International Coaching Federation Certified Coach, Certified High Performance Coach created by Brendon Burchard, and has trained with motivational guru Tony Robbins at his Mastery Levels in Life, Wealth, and Leadership for the past eight years.

Now, Ann has distilled her experience and knowledge into the simple yet highly-effective Wealth Attraction™ Formula, which she shares with entrepreneurs through her Wealth Attraction™ Academy. This formula is a simple yet powerful pathway to creating wealth, success, and fulfillment not only in business, but in life.

Learn more about Ann's programs, services, and educational offerings at WealthAttractionAcademy.com.

www.ingramcontent.com/pod-product-compliance
Lightning Source LLC
LaVergne TN
LVHW021519080426
835509LV00018B/2564